FORTUNE-TELLING BY PALMISTRY

'Up to date and informative . . . a practical guide to this fascinating art.'
— Books to Buy

£2

FORTUNE-TELLING BY PALMISTRY

A Practical Guide to the Art of Hand Analysis

RODNEY DAVIES

THE AQUARIAN PRESS

First published 1987

British Library Cataloguing in Publication Data

Davies, Rodney
Fortune-telling by palmistry
1. Palmistry
I. Title
133.6   BF921

ISBN 0-85030-599-3

*The Aquarian Press is part of the
Thorsons Publishing Group, Wellingborough,
Northamptonshire, NN8 2RQ, England*

Printed and bound in Great Britain by
Mackays of Chatham PLC, Chatham, Kent

7   9   10   8   6

CONTENTS

1

THE HAND AND THE PLANETS

Palmistry or hand reading is an ancient method of character analysis and of divination, whereby the shape, size, colour and proportions of the hand and its parts, and the clarity, length and position of the palm lines, are used to determine human personality and fate.

Hand reading is not a superstition. The modern investigations of Dr Charlotte Wolff, Noel Jaquin, Dr Julius Spier, Dr Theodore Berry and others have conclusively shown that the hands are the living symbols of an individual's health, character and psychological state. And because these are the foundations upon which everyone builds his or her life, the hands can also serve as a guide to how that life will unfold. They can reveal, in other words, the individual's fate or destiny. Indeed, it is the purpose of this book to show you, in an up-to-date and informative way, how to read your own hands and the hands of others.

The human body is a microcosm enshrining the truths of the macrocosm or cosmos. 'As above, so below', read the emerald tablet found clutched in the skeletal hands of Hermes Trismegistus, a revelation that led the sages of old to not only identify everything in nature with the seven planets and the twelve zodiac signs, but to seek the secrets of the stars both in the world around them and in their own bodies.

Your hands therefore are the equivalent of your birth chart. They can tell you all that your chart can and perhaps even more, for they are not based on a half-remembered time of birth or subject to mathematical inaccuracies. They are correct in every detail and are expressive of your nature and fate. They only require interpreting, which is what this book will teach you to do. With it you will soon understand every facet of your character and every twist and turn of your life. And used wisely this knowledge will enable you to take advantage of your strengths and of your favourable periods and minimize the problems resulting from your weaknesses and the difficulties of your unfavourable periods.

But before we get down to specifics we must first consider the hands from a general and astrological point of view. This will help you to understand the many features of hand reading that are dealt with later in the book.

The first seemingly unremarkable, yet most important fact about hands is that we each have two of them. This is because we are bilaterally symmetrical or two-sided creatures. Cut a man or woman down the middle from head to toe and you end up with two parts that are mirror images of each other. In fact even those organs that occur singly have two distinct halves. The brain, for example, has two hemispheres and the heart is divided into a right side and a left side. We are each one, but we are built up of twos.

And yet while we have two hands, few of us are ambidextrous, even though both members of our other organ pairs function with equal facility. In fact some 85 per cent of us are predominantly right-handed, the remainder left-handed. And so it has been throughout recorded history, which is why the majority have concluded that there is something inherently good about the right hand and evil about the left hand. For the left hand is clumsy, awkward and skittish, seemingly possessed of a malevolent nature of its own, while the right hand does what we want it to do; it is amenable to our control.

In the Greek myth recounting the birth of Zeus, the king of the gods, it was said that when Rhea, his mother, went into labour she dug her fingers into the ground and that from the impressions they made sprang ten beings known as the Dactyls, five from those of her right hand and five from those of her left. The right Dactyls were all men who became smiths and the left Dactyls were all women who became witches and the weavers of spells. The names of the women have never been revealed, but those of the men are known. Heracles was the Dactyl of the thumb, Paeonius of the forefinger, Epimedes of the middle finger, Iasius of the third finger, and Acesidas of the pinky or fourth finger.

This myth encapsulates the beliefs that have grown up around the hands. The right hand is the male, good, useful and open hand, the hand of the conscious mind, wakefulness and of life itself. The left hand, contrarily, is female, evil, useless and closed, the hand of the unconscious mind, of secretiveness, and of rest, sleep and death. These opposites form a natural unity, just as the two hands contribute to the wholeness of ourselves.

The hands, like the arms and shoulders, are ruled by the zodiac sign of Gemini and thus by the planet Mercury, whom the Greeks called Hermes. The right hand symbolizes Mercury as an Olympian deity, this being the hand with which we write, strum a musical instrument, throw dice, seal bargains, etc., while the left hand represents Mercury in his guise as conductor of the dead. The number of Mercury is 5, which is the number of digits on a hand, while the alphabet, which Mercury is said to have invented, has five vowels, each of which is identified with one of the fingers: the thumb is linked with vowel A, the forefinger with O, the middle finger with U, the ring finger with E, and the little finger with I.

But although Mercury is given overall rulership of the hands, the parts of the hands are each ruled by one or other of the seven traditional planets, as is shown by Figure 1.

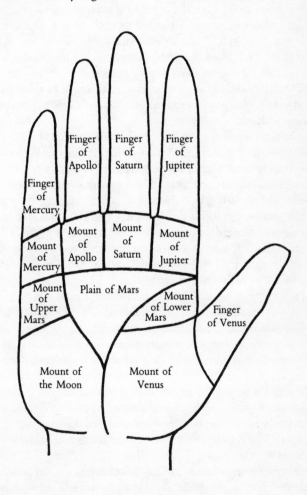

Figure 1

The thumb is ruled by Venus, the forefinger by Jupiter, the middle finger by Saturn, the third finger by the Sun (or Apollo) and the little finger by Mercury. The fleshy ball of the thumb is also ruled by Venus and is known as the mount of Venus. Smaller mounts are found beneath the fingers and each takes its name from the finger above it. The rest of the hand is ruled by the Moon and Mars. The mount of the Moon lies opposite the mount of Venus and runs halfway up the outer side of the palm. The part of the hand ruled by Mars is divided into three, which together comprise the places touched by a sword handle when it is laid across the palm. There is the centrally-placed Plain or Triangle of Mars, and on either side of this lie the two mounts of Mars. The mount placed between the mount of Mercury and the mount of the Moon is called the mount of Upper Mars, the other, that placed atop the mount of Venus, is the mount of Lower Mars (so named because it lies below the Life line).

To understand the traits of character linked with these parts of the hand it is necessary to first examine the natures of the planets with which they are identified.

The seven planets of traditional astrology consist of the two Biblical 'lights' — the Sun and the Moon — and the five bodies which are still classified as planets by modern astronomers: Mercury, Venus, Mars, Jupiter and Saturn. Because they were thought to control human destiny, this in turn gave a special and sacred meaning to the number 7, which became the number of learning, wisdom and occult knowledge. Three more planets are now known — Uranus, Neptune and Pluto — but because there is no general agreement about which areas of the hand they rule, their influence will be ignored for the purposes of this book.

The **SUN** is the largest of the celestial bodies under consideration and is, of course, a star, a vast and incandescent ball of gas, around which orbits the Earth and the other planets and their attendant satellites.

The Sun is traditionally associated with the conscious mind and the ego, and with those positive character traits such as activity, enthusiam, confidence, hopefulness, and physical and sexual vigour. Negatively, it is the planet of rashness, impulsiveness, naivety and a tendency to sulk. Although the Sun-god Helius was very much a deity in his own right in early Greek myth, the Sun later became linked with Apollo, the son of Zeus (or Jupiter) and Leto who became, to all intents and purposes, the Sun-god. This is why the third finger and the mount below it are named after Apollo. Apollo was the god of healing, music and the arts, and of all those other pursuits that can broadly be termed 'civilized', such as philosophy, astronomy, mathematics and science. The two maxims most closely associated with Apollo are 'Know thyself' and 'Avoid excess'.

The Sun has a waxing and a waning phase which occur as a natural part of its daily and yearly cycles. Each morning the Sun climbs above the eastern horizon — 'And Phoebus 'gins arise' — to bring the day, continues to rise to its maximum noon height, and then descends to set below the western horizon. As the Sun climbs, its warming and illuminating effect increases, its waxing phase, while as it descends these decrease, its waning phase.

A similar cycle of increase and decrease takes place during the course of a year. The Sun's waxing phase starts in the northern hemisphere on 21 December, the Winter Solstice, which is the shortest day and when the Sun's noon height is lowest. In the following months the days steadily lengthen and the Sun's noon height increases. By 20 March, the Spring Equinox, the day and night length are equal. The day continues to lengthen until 22 June, the Summer Solstice, when the Sun reaches its maximum noon height. Thereafter the day length shortens and the Sun's noon height decreases, a six-month period that constitutes the Sun's waning phase.

In the hand, the thumb is the digit of the Winter Solstice, when the Sun is reborn. The forefinger is the digit of the Spring Equinox. The middle or Saturn finger is the digit of the Summer Solstice, the third or Apollo finger that of the Autumn Equinox, and the little or Mercury finger is also the digit of the Winter Solstice, when the Sun dies. The Winter Solstice was celebrated throughout the pagan world — the Romans called it the Saturnalia — because it was a time of death and rebirth, which is why Christians chose 25 December as Christ's birthday, the Son replacing the Sun as the object of adoration.

The Sun's waxing phase is identified with the right or positive hand, specifically with the right third finger and its associated mount, and with those positive actions and qualities of human life such as birth, growth, health, wakening, fitness, fleetness of foot, courage, surmounting obstacles, unfolding and openness, and with the brightening of the light. The waning phase, alternatively, is identified with the left or negative hand, especially with the left third finger and its mount, and with those negative actions and qualities like ageing, sickness, loss of vitality, fear, defeat, retreat, retirement, darkness and death.

In a general sense the third fingers and the two Apollo mounts symbolize emotional health, artistic endowment and the desire for worldly success. The right-hand third finger and its mount relate to the outward expression of these, to developed charm and attractiveness and to success attained in an artistic or educational sense, while the left third finger and its mount represent the associated inner qualities, that is, actual emotional health, physical vigour, the capacity for study and practise, the skill in understanding the meaning of an artist's work, and with all the inward-looking aspects of the creative life.

This should make it clear that the terms 'positive' and 'negative' are not to be simply respectively identified with 'good' and 'bad'. They are rather two halves of a whole, the positive being the outer, active half and the negative the inner, passive half. The halves together form the complete person, in the same way that an individual is only whole and normal if he or she has two hands, two eyes, two kidneys, two testicles or ovaries, and so on.

It is important to also appreciate that while the third fingers and the Apollo mounts are linked with the qualities mentioned above, they are not the only parts of the hands that are. And this is why no judgements should be made on the evidence supplied by a single hand part. The secret of accurate hand reading is consensus.

The number of the positive Sun is 1, that of the negative Sun is 4. The Sun's metal is gold and its colours are gold and yellow. A married woman usually wears a gold ring on the third finger of her left hand to show that she has joined her female lunar nature with that of her solar husband.

The **MOON**, the second of the two lights, is apparently identical in shape and size to the Sun, or at least it is when it is full, which is why the ancients believed them to be a pair of watching eyes. The Egyptians, for instance, said that the Sun was the right eye and the Moon the left eye of the divine falcon Horus.

But the Moon is actually a much smaller body than the Sun, being a rocky, not a gaseous sphere, which shines only with the reflected light of the Sun. It appears to be the same size as the Sun only because it is much closer to us.

Astrologically, the Moon — the goddess Selene — is female. In Greek myth Selene was the sister of Helius, the Sun, and of Eos, the Dawn. The Moon grows and diminishes, or waxes and wanes, in a twenty-eight day cycle that mirrors the female menstrual cycle. The waxing Moon is positive, the waning Moon negative. This naturally identifies the waxing Moon with the right-hand Moon mount and the waning Moon with the left-hand Moon mount. The Moon's metal is silver and its colours are white, amber and emerald green. 2 is the number of the waxing Moon, 7 the number of the waning Moon.

And just as Helius became merged with Apollo in later Greek myth, so Selene was associated with Artemis, Apollo's twin sister. Artemis was the Maiden of the Silver Bow, the weapon representing the pale New Moon. Her divine functions were contrary in character, for while she was the goddess of childbirth and the protectress of young children and suckling animals, she was also a huntress who had the power to send plagues and sudden death. These two sides naturally reflected the waxing, growth or life phase of the Moon and its waning, shrinkage or death phase.

The Moon symbolizes the female half of the human psyche and the female sex, in the same way that the Sun stands for the masculine psychical half and the male sex. Thus the Moon represents the unconscious mind, intuition, introversion, inspiration, irrationality, passivity, deception, sleep and dreams, secret things, water and other liquids and darkness. The Moon is also symbolic of the mother, the Sun of the father.

The mounts of the Moon in turn symbolize the positive and negative qualities of the Moon. The right Moon mount is the indicator of imaginative potential, creativity, inspiration, intuition, mysticism and occult interests, while the left Moon mount can signify irritability, abnormal introspection, morbid melancholy or depression, suicidal tendencies, unhealthy imagination and superstition.

The planet closest to the Sun is **MERCURY** which is the smallest of the inner planets. The finger of Mercury is the smallest finger and stands next to the third or solar finger. Space-probe photographs taken of Mercury in the 1970s showed it to be a barren planet pock-marked with craters like the Moon.

In myth, Mercury (or Hermes) was the son of Jupiter and Maia. His mother gave her name to May, the fifth month. The number of Mercury is 5, its metal is quicksilver or mercury, and its colours yellow, orange and light green.

Because Mercury lies so close to the Sun it is usually only possible to see it shortly after sunset. Indeed, Mercury was originally the god of twilight, which is why, this being the time when the world becomes murky and uncertain, Mercury's character was said to be capricious, changeable and dishonest. Mercury was the god of speech and intelligence, music and invention, soothsaying, trade and commerce, treaties, theft and artifice, travel and mathematics. In these respects he was a very active and worldly god. But he was also the messenger of Zeus and, as the god of sleep, he typically delivered his messages in the form of dreams. More ominously, as a god of death, he delivered the souls of the dead to Charon, the ferryman, who rowed them across the black waters of the Styx.

Mercury's positive or Olympian side, representing intelligence, skill in speech, mathematics and science, shrewdness, commercial aptitude and love of travel, is shown by the fourth or little finger of the right hand and by its associated mount, while Mercury's negative or underworld side, that of dishonesty, unfairness and a tendency to lie, cheat and steal, is symbolized by the fourth finger and its mount of the left hand. The little fingers are known as the 'auricular' or 'ear' fingers because both are ideal for cleaning the ears — Greek men still grow a long nail on one of their little fingers to make it more effective in this respect — and because it was thought that by placing these fingers in the ears they would promote inspiration.

VENUS, the second planet from the Sun, takes its name from the goddess of love, whom the Greeks called Aphrodite. It lies at a mean distance of 65 million miles from the Sun and is about the same size as the Earth. Its surface, however, is known to be very hot, due to the greenhouse effect of its cloudy atmosphere. The number of Venus is 6, its metal is copper and its colours are blue, green and violet.

Venus is the brightest object in the sky apart from the Sun and the Moon. It is usually seen either just before sunrise, when it is known as the morning star, or just after sunset, when it is called the evening star. In times past the morning star was named Phospherus and was said to be lucky, while the evening star was named Hesperus and was considered unlucky. Indeed, Venus was known as the 'Star of Lamentation' when it shone at night.

Although we now think of Venus as the delightful and beguiling goddess of love, she originally had two opposite sides to her character, in keeping with her appearances as either the morning star or the evening star. For she was both the benign goddess of love and sexual pleasure and the feared goddess of war, the murderous Lady of Battles. And while her husband was the lame smith Vulcan or Hephaestus, her lover was Mars, the god of war, whom she bore three sons.

The benign or positive aspect of Venus is associated with the thumb and the mount of Venus of the right hand, its malevolent or negative aspect with the thumb and the mount of Venus of the left hand. Thus those traits like warm-heartedness, affection, generosity, sympathy and normal sexual desire are linked with the right hand, specifically in fact with the right Venus mount, while sensuality, vanity, selfishness, loose morals and unnatural pleasures are linked with the left Venus mount. The thumb itself, the digit of Venus, is concerned more with such mental properties as will-power and logic than with our animal instincts, although will-power and reason can of course stop us from being led astray by our desires. Hence the right thumb reveals how we apply our will-power to the world, the left how we apply it to ourselves. Because the thumb allows us to grip and thereby impose our will on nature, its type, position and strength are of great importance in estimating character.

The planet **MARS** is the fourth planet from the Sun, the third being the Earth itself. Known as the 'red planet' because of its red colouring which derives from the iron content of its sands and rocks, Mars thereby became associated with blood and war in the very earliest of times. It is intermediate in size between Mercury and the Earth.

Mars was originally the Roman god of vegetation, the energizing principle that came with the spring in March, the month of Mars, and which caused crops to grow. He was a deity of the forests and mountains as well as the fields, and he also protected cattle from disease. It was only later that he became the god of war. The Greeks called him Ares and gave him a sister named Eris, who started wars by prompting greed, jealousy and suspicion. The number of Mars is 9, its metal is iron and its colours are red and pink.

Martian energy can be either positive or negative and in this sense we see Mars in his most useful or beneficent guise when he was an agricultural deity, the god of germination and growth, and at his most disruptive when he became the god of war. And yet it is controlled aggression that gives us the strength to face up to life, to persevere, to endure and to overcome difficulties and hardships. In a word, such energy gives us courage. Negatively, it can make us violent, insolent, impulsive, uncaring, insensitive, and bloodthirsty or, when lacking completely, timid, shy, hesitant, inferior and frightened.

As we have already seen each hand has three Mars areas, the Upper and Lower Mars mounts and the Plain of Mars. The mount of Lower Mars relates to our aggression, push and drive, the mount of Upper Mars to our capacity to resist and endure, while the Plain of Mars represents our temper. The right-hand Mars areas reveal the outer expressions of these, the left-hand Mars areas the inner ones.

The fifth planet from the Sun is **JUPITER**, the largest planet of the solar system and therefore named after the king of the gods. Jupiter is the first of the gas planets and lies at a mean distance of 480 million miles from the Sun. It takes about twelve Earth years to make one orbit of the parent body.

Jupiter (or Zeus) was the most powerful Olympian deity, the wielder of the thunderbolt and the ruler of the sky. With his two brothers Neptune and Pluto, known to the Greeks as Poseidon and Hades, he governed nature, the other gods and the world of man. The planet Jupiter's number is 3, its metal is tin and its colours are purple and brown.

And yet although Jupiter was worshipped as 'the mighty Father both of God and man', he was also the tyrant who had come to power by dethroning his father Saturn and whose amorous instincts led him to seduce or rape numerous nymphs, goddesses and women. These two sides in turn represent the loving, caring parent and the selfish, arrogant egoist, tendencies that are expressed by the forefingers and the Jupiter mounts, those of the right hand symbolizing the positive attributes of ego and those of the left hand its negative attributes. Thus the Jupiter fingers and their mounts are indicative of personal pride or self-respect, ambition, the capacity to rule and, Jupiter being the supreme deity of the old pantheon, religious belief. We shall see later how the hands show if these important traits are developed normally or not.

Finally, **SATURN**, the ringed planet, is the second largest planet of the solar system. It lies at a mean distance of 886 million miles from the Sun, which it orbits once every 29.5 Earth years. It has ten moons, the most massive of which is Titan, which is bigger than the Moon.

The god Saturn, whom the Greeks called Cronus, rose to power by castrating his father Uranus with a flint sickle. Because Saturn grasped Uranus' genitals with his left hand as he cut them off this explains why the left hand is the hand of ill omen. Astrologically, Saturn is the planet of introversion, conservatism, reservation, reflection, seriousness, old age and death, qualities that all derive from the planet's slow pace through the zodiac and its faint, half-alive glow. In its negative expression Saturn governs failure, misfortune, depression and disappointment.

The middle finger of each hand belongs to Saturn, lying as it does between the thumb and first finger on the one side and the third and fourth fingers on the other. Such a placement necessarily represents the middle course or the Golden Mean. Saturn, like Mars, was originally an agricultural deity, which is suggested by his sickle, and the myth of his castration of Uranus perhaps refers to that period of human history when agriculture was replacing hunting. The Greeks certainly looked back longingly to the 'age of Cronus', when life was easy and the people happy and which ended only when Saturn was usurped by Jupiter, that is, when barbarians from the north overran Greece and conquered the simple agricultural society that had established itself there. The planet Saturn's number is 8, its metal is lead and its colours are black, indigo and grey.

The second finger and its mount reveal one's interest in the outdoors, and in animals, agriculture and horticulture, and similarly one's degree of caution, prudence, sobriety and independence. The right-hand Saturn finger and its mount express the positive Saturn characteristics of clear, analytical thought, the capacity for reflection and balanced judgement, while the left-hand middle finger and its mount show the degree to which the personality is distrustful, discontented, selfish, greedy and fanatical. The negative Saturn person is indifferent to the plight of others, aloof and unfeeling.

Each hand is therefore expressive of a half of ourselves, the right hand revealing our Jungian mask, the side that we display to others, that is, the personality that we wish to project, while the left hand portrays our inner, hidden self, which is frequently as flawed, selfish and gullible as our outer self is correct, altruistic and sensible. The real 'us' is of course both parts, the light and the dark, the perfect and the imperfect, and the mistake we usually make where others are concerned is to believe that the visible tip of the iceberg they show us is 'them', whereas the bulk is concealed beneath waters that are impenetrable to the eye. Hopefully, this book will clear that water somewhat, enabling you to examine both your own muddy depths and those of others. If so, go forward carefully and sensitively.

2

HAND SHAPE AND BASIC CHARACTER

The first Western philosopher of whom we know was Thales of Miletus (flourished sixth century BC), who, grappling to understand the basic reality of the world, concluded that the primary substance was water, which he had doubtlessly observed could exist as a liquid, a solid and a gas. His fellow Ionian Anaximenes disagreed, claiming that air was the underlying cause of things, while Heraclitus said that 'the world is an ever-living fire', which suggested a preference for rapid oxidation.

It was, however, the Sicilian-Greek Empedocles who made the radical proposal that the world was constructed from four 'roots' or elements, Water, Earth, Air and Fire, a notion that persisted for two thousand years and which was only seriously challenged in the eighteenth century.

Empedocles' four elements and their proportions within the human body were held to account for character and temperament. A person with a preponderance of Fire was hot and angry or *choleric*; of Earth, calm and unhurried or *phlegmatic*; of Air, hopeful and amorous or *sanguine*; and of Water, sad and uncertain or *melancholic*. A balanced person necessarily contained equal quantities of the four elements.

This division of personality into four basic types or tendencies is by no means as dead or as old-fashioned as it might seem. Indeed, Carl Jung believed that in reacting to others and to the world around us we each display one of two attitudes and one of four functions. The two attitudes are the familiar introversion, an inward-looking, passive mode, and extroversion, an outward-looking, active mode, while the four Jungian functions are Thinking, Feeling, Sensation and Intuition.

And yet although we are used to classifying ourselves as either introverts or extroverts, we know that our reactions vary according to the circumstances of the moment, so that a quiet type may become relatively open and talkative at times and the bold type shy and withdrawn. Hence while our basic tendency may be introvert or extrovert, we are never locked exclusively into that mode.

The same can be said of the four functions. The Thinking function takes place when we use our brains analytically, as when we are trying to understand how something works, the Feeling function when we are judging things in their totality, as wholes rather than the sum of their parts. Jung termed these two functions 'rational'. The two ' irrational' functions of Sensation and Intuition differ in that the Sensation function is one of basic awareness, of seeing things without judging them, while the Intuition function extracts an inner meaning from what is being observed.

It is not hard to see a similarity between Jung's four functions and the four temperament types that derive from a preponderance of one or other of the four elements. Thus Air is a synonym for the Thinking function, Fire for the Feeling function, Earth for the Sensation function, and Water for the Intuition function.

Furthermore, Jung's two attitudes of introversion and extroversion closely match what we have learned of the left and right hands. The left hand, being the hand that is clumsy, awkward and feminine, is the Introverted hand and the poised, adept and masculine right hand is the Extroverted hand. The left hand is thus expressive of our inner nature and of our inherited potential or genotype, the right hand of our outer selves and of our developed persona or phenotype.

The Jungian function with which we are more comfortable and which represents our basic character is shown by the shape of our hands, this being determined by the squareness or otherwise of the palms and by the length of the fingers.

To determine your hand shape first measure the width and the length of your palms. If these measurements are the same or approximately the same, your palm is SQUARE. If your palms, however, are longer than their width they are RECTANGULAR. It is important to notice if one palm is more square or more rectangular than the other.

Next, compare the lengths of your fingers, notably that of the middle fingers, with the palm lengths. If your fingers are shorter than your palms, they are SHORT. If they are as long or longer than your palms, they are LONG.

These simple measurements give four hand shapes. First, the square palm with short fingers. Second, the square palm with long fingers. Third, the rectangular palm with short fingers and, fourth, the rectangular palm with long fingers. The first is the Earth or Sensation hand, the second the Air or Thinking hand, the next the Fire or Feeling hand, and the last the Water or Intuition hand. The character type associated with these hand shapes is described below.

The Earth Hand (Square palm and short fingers)

To the ancients the element Earth, represented by the ground beneath their feet, was the foundation upon which rested the surrounding spheres of water, air and fire. It was solid, strong and enduring, the cornerstone of the universe. In it grew the plants of the field and on it lived both animals and man. Indeed, Genesis says that 'the Lord God formed man of the dust of the ground and breathed into his nostrils the breath of life'. Thus we are all products of the element Earth.

But the earth can and does move. Long-term tectonic movements can bring great changes to any landscape, sometimes pushing mountains up to the very heights of heaven. Short-term, sudden movements also occur and when they do, as when a volcano erupts or an earthquake splits and shakes the ground, the destruction is widespread and catastrophic. This makes the earth both a steady friend and, on occasions, a treacherous enemy.

The Earth individual is the human expression of the element Earth. If your hands are of this type you are a stable and practical person, who does not like to be hurried and who prefers to go with the current rather than swim against it. You are honest, fair-minded and conservative, and you have a good measure of common sense. You don't give your affection or your loyalty very easily, but once you do they are given to last.

You do not have a fast-working, intellectual mind. It takes you time to make decisions and to understand things that are at all complicated. This is why you both work and study best when you can proceed at your own pace. But you do have an excellent memory, which is why forgetting past wrongs is so hard for you. And yet while such hurts can have a souring effect on you if you let them, your attitude to life is generally quietly optimistic.

You are happiest when you know where you are and where you're going. Uncertainty upsets you, as does sudden and unexpected change. Ideally, you need to be able to set your own goals and then work towards them cautiously and single-mindedly. You find the idea of overnight success intrinsically abhorent as you cannot value anything that you have not had to sweat for.

Your unadventurous nature makes you a stay-at-home, careful sort of person, who is happy with the known and the familiar and suspicious of the foreign and the different. This is why you love and revere the past, when life was seemingly simpler and more straightforward. You prefer work that is practical and somewhat repetitious, especially if it gets you outdoors and involves the land or natural materials. You also like working with animals. But you are materialistic and you believe that a labourer is worthy of his hire. It is probably only the poor pay that stops you from actually working on a farm, but you do like to get out into the garden. Earth people tend to work in high-paying, manual occupations like mining, building, factory work, navvying, etc.

And yet this does not mean that Earth people are only hewers of wood and drawers of water because many have artistic talents of a high order. You may well be musical and have a good singing voice, and you may also be either interested in or a dabbler in wood carving, sculpture, pottery or painting. Practical hobbies like knitting, sewing, cooking, dress making and furniture making similarly appeal to you. Earth types also enjoy sports that are rough and energetic. They make keen and talented boxers, wrestlers, footballers and rugby players.

You are sympathetic to trade unions and you believe that money should be earned. Thus you tend to be hostile to the moneyed class, unless of course you happen to belong to it yourself. In which case you may be something of a blimp.

You do not possess, however, a revolutionary nature. You much prefer to muddle along with what you know and understand, even though your conditions of life may not be of the best. Yet when you are pushed too far you suddenly flare up and become a stubborn, aggressive opponent, awesome in your destructive power. But in ordinary times you have a strong sense of right and wrong and you believe very firmly in law and order. Indeed, you instinctively understand that civilization is based upon fair play and decent behaviour.

The Air Hand (Square palm and long fingers)
The element Air is very different from Earth. It is invisible, insubstantial and impossible to grasp. Yet it is essential to life as all living things, both plants and animals, require the oxygen it contains. And yet air is the medium in which many creatures spend much of their lives, and those that do, like birds, bats and insects, are quick and active. Air also carries sound waves and is the medium through which radio and television signals pass. The air constantly makes its presence felt in the form of breezes and winds, or sometimes as destructive hurricanes. It also brings water in the form of rain, hail and snow.

Unlike the Earth type, the Air individual enjoys using his or her mind. If you belong to this group you love absorbing new facts, studying for examinations and keeping abreast of what is going on in the world. You likewise need to talk and to share your ideas and opinions with others. And you welcome intellectual challenges, whether these be in the form of games like chess or an occupation which requires thought and analysis, such as computing and scientific research.

You are an independent soul who is happiest when you are doing your own thing. You work best on your own, although you can function well in a team if the others look up to you. Your bright confidence derives from your intellectual ability, which is why you always need to keep your mind honed. To you, knowledge is power.

But you're neither very practical nor interested in working with your hands. Yet because you can see how things should be done, you make a competent organizer and teacher. You love to pore over maps and plans, interpreting them and telling others what to do. Your desired title is 'Director of Operations'.

You tend, however, to be unpredictable and contrary, and changing your mind is something you do frequently and without embarrassment. This is why you don't get on very well with Earth people, who seem to you to be too slow and set in their ways. But while you have an active and enquiring mind, you have trouble in connecting with your emotions. In fact you are rather frightened of your feelings and of the irrational pressures that these produce. This is why your enthusiasm often lacks warmth and why you're often considered to be a bit of a cold fish, unsympathetic and uptight.

You look down on those whose wits are less agile than your own and who don't have your easy command of words. Your intellectual smugness can make you caustic and disagreeable, prompting you to sometimes dismiss another's problems with a sniff and a snide 'Well, it's her own fault. She wouldn't be in such a mess if she'd done this, this and that'. But because human relationships are based on more than intellect, your interactions with others are usually less than ideal.

Because Air types love uncovering facts and sharing them with the world, they are attracted to work in the media and in education. Quite probably you are either employed as a teacher or journalist, or have considered such work, or you make your bread as a public relations consultant, writer, psychiatrist, researcher, scientist, detective, presenter and so on. Unlike the Earth person you dislike work that is dirty or dull or repetitious or which is mainly physical.

You are very much inclined to get bees in your bonnet, to become quite fanatical in your beliefs, which is why you may be a food faddist, an anti-smoker, a health freak, a ban-the-bomber, a women's liberationist, an animal rights activist or a vegetarian. In this respect you can try and limit the rights of others and so go against your professed belief in freedom. One of life's little ironies, no less.

The Fire Hand (Rectangular palm and short fingers)
Fire is the most active and energizing of the four elements, the one that

can both stimulate and destroy. Fire is hot and constantly moving, and its control and use was the singlemost important advance in man's evolution. But while useful and beneficial, uncontrolled fire is one of the most destructive forces in nature. To the ancients, Fire was divine and the element closest to heaven.

The Fire individual is marked out by his or her energy and enthusiasm. If you belong to this group you are restless, outgoing and ambitious. You don't like standing still in whatever you do. In fact you want to rise in the world, to achieve and become successful. You believe in getting out there and going for what you want. Ever onwards and upwards is your approach to life.

As with the Air person you dislike authority and you are always happy to cock your nose at it. You thrive on excitement and adventure, which is why you enjoy travelling, taking risks and generally doing what you shouldn't. You're the sort who drives too fast, drinks too much and who burns—what else?—the midnight oil. In fact in your pure form you're very much the happy-go-lucky, devil-may-care extrovert, the kind of guy or gal who, in times gone by, rode the range, shot from the hip and robbed the Denver stage.

You get on well with others, perhaps the best of the four hand-shape types. It's true that you're rather big-headed and loud-mouthed, but you're also warm and sympathetic and you like to laugh. Your caring nature prompts you to quickly take up cudgels for the downtrodden and oppressed, especially if you can gain a little kudos in the process.

But while you're a good starter, a pioneer if you like, you tend to burn yourself out rather fast, so losing your energy and enthusiasm. This is why you're best at tackling those schemes and projects that can be finished quickly or which you can hand over to others to complete. You lack the necessary stubborness and tenacity for the long fight, and you're quickly bored. You have a talent, however, for grasping the essence of any problem, of seeing what needs to be done, yet you can get impatient with the details and the finer points. Thus you can see the wood but not the trees.

And just as fire needs air to burn, so you find yourself most at ease with Air people, who complement you. Indeed, because Air types like dealing with the nitty-gritty, they can best handle those areas that bore and irritate you. You are least compatible with Water people, who not surprisingly have a dampening effect on you.

You like to be in the spotlight, to be at the centre of things and where the action is. You're often a trendsetter yourself and you certainly follow fashion and the latest fads. You enjoy going to parties and dances that are noisy and lively, especially as you love contributing to the fun.

Your natural self-confidence and assertiveness has you taking the lead where the opposite sex is concerned. Indeed, your interest in sex and variety can make you promiscuous.

Your need for attention draws you to those jobs that put you in the public eye, which explains why Fire people are often found in politics, sport and entertainment, or in those fields that allow them to champion the rights of others, such as law and labour relations.

You dislike being alone and your desire for company can sometimes get you into trouble, bringing you as it so often does into contact with the wrong sort of people. You are rather selfish and you can be aggressive and demanding, most notably in your dealings with the slower and more cautious Earth and Water types.

The Water Hand (Rectangular palm and long fingers)
Water is a cold, still and fluid element, which while passive in itself can be turned into an angry and destructive force by the tides and the winds. It has no shape of its own but naturally assumes that of its container. Water is forever trying to run away and escape, and it will, if the conditions are sufficiently soft and absorptive, soak itself into that which would otherwise give it support. In moderate amounts water moistens and gives life to the soil, but when present in excessive quantities it floods and drowns. Water also bends light, so distorting anything it covers, while its depths are often dark and unknown. And just as still waters run deep, so a storm may leave untroubled the depths beneath.

If you are a Water person you are quiet, reserved and diffident. You probably don't have any burning ambitions but are, like the element Water, content to remain where you are until acted upon by events or other people. Thus you are not pushy or a go-getter, preferring as you do a rather homely and humdrum existence. Your diffidence and caution is caused by your lack of confidence, and this is why it is important for you to live in a stable, familiar environment that protects you from the buffetings of life. In this respect you belong to the most sensitive and psychologically fragile of the four hand-shape types. Your nature makes you most compatible with the honest, solid Earth person, and least compatible with the outgoing and changeable Air and Fire types.

You have a very rich inner life and a good imagination, so much so that your fantasies may seem more real than reality. At worst you are a dreamer, a builder of castles in the air, while at best you are a vivid and colourful story-teller and a weaver of spells. You quite possibly possess creative talents, but if you do you have trouble in focussing your energies to do anything with them. This is why you need help from someone stronger, a Svengali, to produce solid, saleable goods.

Your introversion makes you withdraw from the world, which is encouraged by your imagination as this both magnifies the world's dangers and at the same time gives you a safe, controllable and interesting inner refuge. You require constant encouragement if you are to surmount your anxiety and insecurity, and you too easily give up if you face criticism and opposition.

Because you are so sensitive it doesn't take much to make you despondent and your despondency can lead to both depression and paranoia, a belief that outside forces are conspiring against you. It is not unusual for Water people to feel sad and unhappy, yet their depression can lead them to abuse their bodies with drink and drugs, and sometimes to attempt suicide. Part of your problem is that you tend to blame yourself for your so-called weaknesses and for whatever goes wrong in your life, and these thoughts can have you denigrating yourself as unworthy, weak and useless. This is why it is important for you to stay away from drink and mind-altering drugs, and to make friends with those who have sunny, optimistic temperaments, who can help bring you out of yourself and give you a lift. If anything, you need more laughter in your life.

But although you are inclined to be over-critical of your failings, your intuition and natural sensitivity gives you a good understanding of others, a talent that the more intellectually inclined Air and Fire types find quite mysterious. And because you are a sympathetic listener you are well-equipped to counsel and advise, which is why you are drawn to nursing, social work, psychiatry, veterinary science, chiropody, chiropracty and similar pursuits. Indeed, helping other people solve their difficulties enables you to rise above your own. You are also attracted to any work that has to do with the sea and with liquids. You tend, however, to be too critical and to complain too much.

You may possess extra-sensory powers and with training you could become a capable medium or clairvoyant. Your sixth sense can give you warnings and insights that are not available to the other types.

The foregoing character descriptions should make it plain that the Air and Fire types, who are concerned with the control of others and their environment, are rational and extroverted in a Jungian sense, while the Earth and Water types, who are more concerned with their inner selves and with keeping in step with natural rhythms, are irrational and introverted.

But this only describes their basic tendency, for in reality those belonging to these four groups can either be introverted or extroverted themselves. Thus the four types become eight when this attitude factor is considered. You may therefore be an Introverted Earth type or an Extroverted Earth type, an Introverted Air type or an Extroverted Air type, an Introverted Fire type or an Extroverted Fire type, or an Introverted Water type or an Extroverted Water type.

Your attitude is revealed by your dominant hand. If you are right-handed you have an extroverted tendency and if you are left-handed you have an introverted tendency. Thus if you have rectangular palms and short fingers, yet use your left hand, you are an Introverted Fire type, while if you have square palms and short fingers, but are right-handed, you are an Extroverted Earth type.

Most people are of course either Extroverted Earth, Air, Fire or Water types, due to the fact that the majority is right-handed. The left-handed Introverts form a generally despised minority group, whose practical needs are seldom catered for and whose special way of looking at the world is largely ignored. Those few who are ambidextrous are the most fortunate, being naturally more balanced.

Your brain is divided into a right hemisphere and a left hemisphere. The right hemisphere, oddly enough, controls the left side of the body, the left hemisphere its right side. Thus if you are right-handed you use the left side of your brain more than its right side, while if you are left-handed the reverse is true. And because the left hemisphere is concerned with analytic, logical thinking and with verbal and linear functioning in general, while the right hemisphere operates far more holistically, being concerned with spatial orientation, face and object recognition, artistic endeavour and body image, this explains why right-handedness and left-handedness reveal introversion or extroversion. Thus the right-handed person is the analyser and the doer, the type who wants to impose his or her will on the world, the extrovert, and the left-handed person is the artist and interpreter, the type who seeks harmony with the world, the introvert.

This added dimension does not alter what has been said about the basic character of the four hand-shape types, but rather refines it. An Extroverted Earth person, for example, is still introverted when compared with an Introverted Fire person, yet he or she deals with the world in a different way from an Introverted Earth person.

To make this clearer let us consider two council workers, one an Extroverted Earth type, the other an Introverted Earth type, who have just completed preparing a cricket pitch for the weekend match. As both look the pitch over, the Extroverted worker admires the flatness and greenness of the turf, the whiteness and geometrical precision of the markings, and its general fitness for the game soon to be played on it. His Introverted co-worker, however, becomes wrapped up in the images that the colours and the layout of the pitch generate within him. The greenness suggests freshness, life and vitality, the white markings wholesomeness, honour and playing the game, the whole intimating divine order, that God created the world so that men would one day play cricket upon it.

An Extroverted Air person in the same way relates his many ideas to the world about him, giving them a value which stems from their usefulness. He is, in this sense, the applied mathematician, making use of a system to improve his environment. The Introverted Air type, conversely, is the pure mathematician, who is concerned solely with ideas and not with their practical application or with their relation to external objects. For him, ideas are an end in themselves, but for his extroverted colleague they are a means to an end.

The Fire person, as we have seen, is concerned with value, with judging things and getting the best out of them. The Extroverted Fire person puts value on objects and people, which is why he or she finds it easy to establish relationships with others. The Introverted Fire type is concerned with inner values, thus his or her activity in the world has much to do with self-fulfilment and achieving personal satisfaction. Such values are often hard to explain to others, as are the feelings which accompany them.

Lastly, the Extroverted Water person wants to understand the inner cause of external events or why things happen as they do and to uncover the motives of others and to see where their behaviour leads them. The Introverted Water type seeks to understand the workings of his or her own mind, to peer into his inner depths and dredge about among his fears, drives and desires, and to work out what goals they are pointing him towards.

3

THE THUMBS

The thumb and the four fingers make each hand the useful and most human body part that it is. The hands enable us to hold and to manipulate objects, thereby permitting us to impose our will on nature. For without hands we could not have become the dominant animals that we are. Dolphins, for example, have brains as large and as intelligent as our own, yet without hands they are unable to use their abilities as purposefully and as self-assertively as we can. Such dominance may eventually lead to our downfall, but there can be no doubt that our hands have given us the power to realise our dreams.

The hands are as efficient as they are because the thumb truly opposes the fingers, so allowing us to grip, while their musculature and nervous control allows us to carry out delicate and properly co-ordinated movements. Our hands are nothing less than living miracles, which we too often abuse, using them as we do for destructive striking and throwing rather than for creative expression.

We have already discovered that the thumb is the digit of Venus, the forefinger that of Jupiter, the middle finger of Saturn, the third finger of Apollo and the fourth finger of Mercury. It is no coincidence that the thumb bears the name of a goddess and that the fingers are named after gods. Venus, after all, was the goddess of desire, which explains why the four male fingers lean towards her when the hand is closed. Nor is it a coincidence that the thumb can be most easily applied to the tip of the middle or Saturn finger, for in myth Saturn was the creator of Venus, growing as she did from the genitals of Uranus, which Saturn cut off with his flint sickle and threw into the sea.

Each digit is formed from three articulating bones known as the phalanges. This includes the thumb, even though the lowermost phalanx of the thumb is effectively part of the palm and is called the mount of Venus. The first phalanx of each finger is the one bearing the nail, the second phalanx lies in the middle and the third phalanx adjoins the palm.

The length, width and shape of the phalanges are important indicators of character.

The Dactyl of the right thumb is called Heracles, the strong one, the 'glory of Hera'. And each thumb's strength derives not only from its thickness and musculature, but from its ability to oppose the fingers and produce a grip. A hand docked of its thumb is weak and useless.

The best way to begin evaluating your thumbs is to turn your palms towards you and straighten out your fingers, and then to open your thumbs as far from the side of the hands as they can go. You may be able to open them to ninety degrees, so that they form a right angle with the palm. Or you may be able to open your thumbs to an angle greater than ninety degrees or, conversely, you may not be able to open them to ninety degrees. This distance of opening gives three thumb types: the acute thumb, which cannot be opened to ninety degrees; the right-angled thumb which can; and the obtuse thumb that can be opened more than ninety degrees.

The significance of these distances of thumb opening becomes immediately clear if we note that a baby, whose ego has not properly formed, encloses its thumb with its fingers and so hides them away, and that such thumb concealment in an adult is a sign of chronic anxiety, lack of self-esteem and a fear of the outside world. Thus the distance to which the thumbs can be opened is a measure of our confidence and self-worth.

If your thumbs are of the acute type you have doubts about yourself and your abilities, thus you lack confidence. This means that you won't stray too far from what you know and feel secure with, so you'll tend to stick to your home turf. Any type of change worries you and you are reluctant to try new things. In your work, as in your relationships, you stick to the middle ground, to the tried and the true, which means that you're conservative, a lover of custom and tradition, and an upholder of law and order. At best, you're an honest and upright creature of habit; at worst, a blinkered, stubborn reactionary, the type Americans call a redneck. Your caution won't stop you from functioning effectively in your own alley, but it will prevent you from tasting adventure and it could have you missing that big opportunity when it comes your way. You're loyal to your family and friends, but suspicious of and rather hostile to strangers and newcomers. Your attitude to life naturally stems from your lack of self-esteem and from your fear of what could happen to you if you're not careful.

But although this description of the character traits of those having acute thumbs is true in a general sense, it is of course modified by the degree to which the thumbs can open. Hence the smaller the angle of opening, the greater is the fear of the world and the lower the self-esteem. As the angle of opening increases so more confidence is revealed. Thus if your thumbs open to eighty-five degrees, then you will have much in common with the right-angled types.

If your thumbs can open to form a right angle with your palms they show that you have few doubts about yourself. Your self-esteem is high and you possess an independent and adventurous spirit. You welcome change if it brings improvement, thus you don't hanker for the past or fear what tomorrow may bring. And you will take risks, although they will always be calculated risks. You're interested in travel as you like some variety and excitement in your life. This means that in most respects you are balanced and sensible, confident but not over-confident, adventurous but not reckless, independent but not misanthropic. You also speak your mind and you're not afraid of learning new skills. You probably live or would like to live away from your native town, work in a job that interests you and which offers some chance of advancement, and have one or more hobbies that are somewhat out of the ordinary, such as skiing, bird watching or karate.

The third type of thumb is obtuse and can open to an angle greater than ninety degrees. Should your thumbs be of this sort then you don't lack confidence or verve. In fact very little deters you, and if your thumbs open to a wide angle then your high opinion of yourself and your abilities verges on arrogance. You like to be constantly on the move, trying new things and going from one high to the next. Indeed, you love behaving outrageously and shocking people. And because you enjoy taking risks and rising to any challenge it is easy for you to embroil yourself in dangerous activities. In fact you never really know when to stop, when enough's enough. Thus you can, if you're not careful, be offensive and boring in your attitudes, endanger your health through overindulgence and fail by taking too many unnecessary risks. And your conceit can make you shallow and dishonest. But you are blissfully outgoing, good company and lively fun, and you seldom get depressed. You just need to learn when to apply the brake.

These aspects of character must be related to the shape of the hands themselves. Because Water types, for example, are naturally shy and lacking in confidence, a Water person with acute thumbs is more diffident and unassertive than a Fire person with such thumbs (given that the degree of thumb opening is the same), because Fire types are blessed with a more confident basal make-up. Similarly, a Fire person with obtuse thumbs is more headstrong and reckless than an Earth person with such thumbs, the natural caution of the Earth character acting as a brake. The scale with regard to confidence and drive runs from the

Water type, which has the least, through the Earth type, the Air type and, lastly, the Fire type, which has the most. Thus for those possessing acute thumbs the most withdrawn and fearful are the Water types, while those least affected are the Fire types, and for those with obtuse thumbs the most reckless are the Fire types and the least reckless are the Water types.

The next thumb feature of importance to examine is the setting of the thumbs on the hands. Are your thumbs low-set, high-set or middle-set? Their setting is related to their degree of opening as, in general, high-set thumbs can open less widely than low-set thumbs.

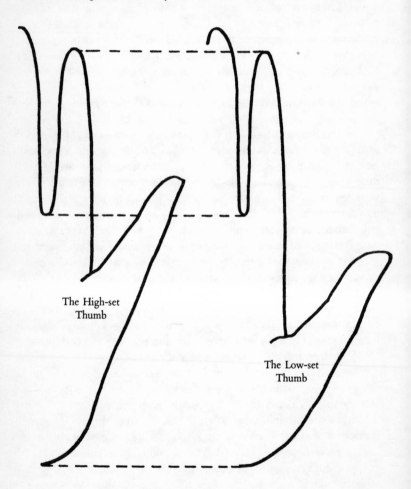

The High-set
Thumb

The Low-set
Thumb

Figure 2

If your thumbs are high-set you are a cautious and uncertain sort of person, one possessed of a mind that does not readily welcome new ideas and which lacks what might be called generous impulses. Your first concern is yourself and all that you do has but one objective, to benefit yourself and your interests. You seldom take risks, preferring instead to tread a narrow path through life. You are, however, capable of hard work and you press on with things stubbornly and single-mindedly. You have an instinctive mistrust of anything strange and novel, and you don't much care for change of any sort. You are more concerned with day-to-day, ordinary matters than with those that are unusual or philosophical, and you have a certain contempt for people who let their minds wander in this sense. You are not imaginative or artistic to any degree, but you do have more than your fair share of common sense. You are a closed person and you keep your thoughts and plans to yourself. You are happiest when you are adding to your stock of wordly goods, although you sense that there is something lacking in your life that you can't quite put your finger on, but which you one day hope to understand and satisfy.

A low-set thumb is an indicator of a freer, more open and confident spirit. If your thumbs are of this type you have a warm and generous nature, a vitality that readily communicates itself to others and which makes you popular. You like to tell jokes and laugh, and nothing gets you down for long. You are free with your possessions and your time, thus you're not backward in paying for your round of drinks. Indeed, you have a sociable disposition and a love of good company, which means that if you possess Fire hands you'll be very much the life and soul of the party type, the jolly extrovert. Your lack of caution, however, can lead you astray, prompting you to do things that are dangerous to yourself and to society at large. And your breezy, irresponsible attitude to life may damage your chances of career success and cause upset to your family. At your best you are happy-go-lucky, ebullient and charming, yet when you do trip yourself up on your coat-tails you become, at your worst, the broken down, whining dipsomaniac, the sort of person that nobody wants to know.

These two character sketches refer to the two ends of a spectrum, the high-set thumb type being one end and the low-set thumb type the other. A thumb which is middle-set naturally indicates a character that falls between these two extremes and thus the sort of person who is more moderate and centred. The setting of the thumbs must also be related to the hand type. A high setting will add a measure of control and thoughtfulness to Air and Fire hands, whose basic character disposition lies in the other direction, while low-set thumbs will reveal a very unstable and irresponsible personality. In a similar manner, a low thumb setting on Earth and Water hands shows that the person concerned is more open and extroverted than might at first be suspected, whereas high-set thumbs mean that the character is surrounded by walls of suspicion and fear and whose concerns are very inwardly-directed.

The degree of opening of the thumbs and their setting must also be related to handedness. Because right-handedness indicates a more logical and outgoing or extroverted attitude, this is necessarily emphasized by low-set, wide-opening thumbs and diminished by high-set, acute thumbs. Left-handedness, however, reveals an intuitive and inward-looking or introverted attitude. This is naturally more extreme if the thumbs are high-set and if they cannot be opened very far, yet less so if they are low-set and obtuse.

Thumb size is likewise important in estimating character, thus you should next determine that of your own. Are they large, medium or small in size? The size of your thumbs is determined by comparing them with the overall size of your hands, because although the thumbs of a large person may well be bigger than those of someone smaller, the first may actually have small thumbs judged by his or her hand size and the second may have large thumbs. In this respect it will help if you take a look at the thumbs of your relatives and friends as this will show you how much thumb size compared with hand size can vary. It will be helpful, too, to see how well their thumb size and what you know about their character accords with what is said below.

Because the thumbs allow us to grip and so impose our will upon the world, they necessarily symbolize our personal force or will-power, our inner strength. The connection between the thumbs and will-power is implicit in the phrase 'under my thumb', which of course means that a person or a situation is under one's control. Hence the larger the thumbs the greater is one's determination and character strength. Large thumbs therefore reveal a desire to dominate, which is the expression of an outgoing, practical and forceful attitude to life. Hand readers have long recognized that it is the large-thumbed who rule the world and that the small-thumbed hear and obey. Napoleon, Hitler, Joseph Stalin, Winston Churchill, Ronald Reagan and Margaret Thatcher all had or have large thumbs. Small thumbs betray a lack of will-power and resolve and in turn an inability to get things done. But although someone with small thumbs is flawed in this sense, he or she may well possess a sensitivity and an artistic talent that the large-thumbed person does not have.

Both large-thumbed and small-thumbed people can have difficulties with their personal relationships, the former because they tend to be too selfish and dominating, the latter because their lack of drive prevents them from pushing themselves forward and looking after their needs. All too often those with small thumbs get overlooked or trodden on.

This naturally suggests that medium-sized or balanced thumbs are the ideal and this is certainly true where personal happiness is concerned. Such thumbs reveal will-power but not an excess of it and sufficient drive to function in the world without wanting to dominate it. Medium-sized thumbs indicate that their owners can both share and stand up for themselves, which suggests that they are likely to be happier in their relationships than those with large or small thumbs.

The thumb as a digit is divided into two phalanges, the first or nail phalanx and the second phalanx which joins the mount of Venus. The length and thickness of these show how you use your mental powers.

Ideally, the length of both phalanges should be about equal. Character imbalances are shown by inequalities of length.

The nail phalanx symbolizes, in a general sense, those aspects of character that are represented by the size of the thumb itself. That is, it reveals will-power, determination and resolve, and hence the ability to lead or command. The second phalanx symbolizes the reasoning capacities, the power to think both logically and sensibly, and thus the power of judgement. Balance in these two areas is essential if one is to behave appositely, for if, by way of example, one's will is strong but reasoning capacity weak, one's life may be spent in chasing rainbows.

A longer first phalanx, especially if this is thick or bulbous, reveals a strong, stubborn wilfulness, a desire to press ahead regardless of the consequences. If your thumbs have longer first phalanges you possess tunnel vision where your ambitions are concerned, which means that you tend to expend energy on pursuing goals that more reasoned thought would have rejected as impractical at best and foolish at worst. Your stubbornness provokes disagreement and argument with those around you, which is made worse by the fact that you find it almost impossible to back down or to say that you're sorry. You function most effectively where there are straightforward rules, yet you can be a real troublemaker when you decide that you want to change the system.

In this respect the clubbed or bulbous thumb is a special case because it is a sign of abnormal obstinacy. When such thumbs are linked with other negative hand features like pronounced Triangles of Mars, indicating a fierce temper, then they betoken a difficult and dangerous person. In traditional palmistry such thumbs were called 'murderer's thumbs', as they are often, although not always, present on the hands of violent criminals. People with thumbs of this type should be treated with caution.

The second phalanx of the thumbs marks our ability to think and reason logically. When it matches the first phalanx in length it reveals that will-power and the logical faculties are in balance with one another, suggesting that the judgement is sound. The will in this case flows from the reason instead of governing it.

If your second phalanges are shorter than the nail phalanges this indicates that your reason is subservient to your will, which reveals that you embark on projects without thinking them through and that you attempt to satisfy your desires without understanding what the consequences will be. Such headstrong behaviour naturally leads you into difficulties and encourages you to make frequent mistakes, unless of course you can learn to seek sensible advice and take it. It goes without saying that criminals often possess deficient second thumb phalanges.

Longer second phalanges, especially if they are markedly longer than the first, denote both a lack of will-power and an excess of reason. Should your thumbs have second phalanges of this type then you are cautious and thoughtful and you are reluctant to make changes too quickly. Such long second phalanges also show that you are cut off from your emotions, which you seek to dominate intellectually. This suggests that you are repressed in one way or another and this is certainly true if your hands are of the Earth or Water type. However, long second phalanges on Fire and Air hands are a sign that the character is more cautious than might otherwise be expected.

Thumb thickness is also important in judging character. In general, a thicker thumb accentuates its properties. Thus thick nail phalanges suggest that the will-power is bolstered by stubbornness. Long, thick nail phalanges are therefore a sign of intractable obstinacy, while thin nail phalanges reveal a will that is easily exhausted. Thick second phalanges are suggestive of an overly-cautious disposition and belong to the person who may not act until it is too late. Short, thick second phalanges are possessed by those who are stubbornly persistent, their will dominating their reason and so preventing them from perceiving their own errors. Long, thick second phalanges indicate a preoccupation with detail and thus slow and cautious movement. Such obsessiveness of character often turns those who have it into hoarders or collectors. If the second phalanges are short and thin, logic and good judgement are lacking. But if the phalanges are long and thin they reveal a refined intellect, their owners being sensitive to the ideas and needs of others.

4

THE FINGERS

The **INDEX** or first finger is named after Jupiter, the Cloud-Gatherer and the Loud-Thunderer, no doubt because it is the most manipulative of the four. Large objects are held by all four fingers opposing the thumb, but small objects are invariably picked up by the thumb and forefinger alone. The Dactyl of the right-hand first finger was named Paeonius or 'deliverer from evil', who also bore the title of Damnameneus or 'hammerer'. Heracles, the Dactyl of the thumb, was likewise titled Acmon or 'anvil', and these names derive from the fact that the forefinger can be stubbed against the thumb in the manner of a hammer being knocked against an anvil, while the second finger can be pushed inbetween to represent an ingot of hot iron. Epimedes, the Dactyl of the second finger, bore the title Celmis, meaning 'smelting'.

In hand analysis the forefingers represent the ego or self, which is why their length and shape and that of their phalanges symbolize how we view ourselves.

The first step in evaluating your own forefingers is to see whether or not they are of normal length. And while admitting that the estimation of finger length can be tricky—after all, is the finger under consideration long or is the one next to it short?—we can in general say that the forefingers are of normal length if they reach to the mid-point of the first phalanx of the second finger beside them or, in other words, to the base of its nail. If your forefingers are longer than this they are long, if shorter they are short. It is important to note if there is any difference in length between your left forefinger and your right forefinger.

If your forefingers are short your evaluation of yourself is low, which means that you suffer from an inferiority complex, the size of which is proportional to the shortness of the fingers. Such a low self-view is necessarily a handicap to finding happiness because no matter what you achieve you will always feel that it isn't enough, thus your life may become a madcap scramble to nowhere. You may behave pushily and assertively, so compensating for your supposed inadequacies by a belligerent manner, or you may bend to your inferiority feelings and be shy, submissive and withdrawn. Neither attitude can of course give you real peace of mind.

Long forefingers indicate a superiority complex. If you possess such fingers you believe you are special and have out-of-the-ordinary gifts, the size of these feelings being again proportional to the length of your forefingers. Because you overvalue your abilities, you tend to trip yourself up by trying to achieve more than you can, which brings disappointment and frustration. Alternatively, you may fail to study or try as hard as you should due to the fact that you so often believe that your knowledge is adequate and that success should come to you by divine right. Your egoism also creates problems for you socially, which contributes to your basic unhappiness.

The Jupiter fingers, like the others, should ideally be straight and well formed. Straight fingers indicate that the qualities associated with them are correctly developed in the sense that their direction is right, whereas bent or twisted fingers are symbolic of psychological imbalance or deviance. Thus the degree of bending or twist is expressive of the amount of imbalance.

It is quite common to find Jupiter fingers that bend or lean towards the middle fingers. And as the middle fingers symbolize our conscience such bending represents the ego's attempts to shelter beneath the conscience or to satisfy its demands. Hence if your Jupiter fingers bend like this it reveals that you set high and rather strict standards for yourself, which makes you a person of some principle, and that in order to achieve what you feel you ought to, you show great determination and single-mindedness, traits that others may interpret as selfishness but which are really the result of you obeying those inner instructions to 'Be good' or 'Do well' or whatever. The degree of bending of the fingers will therefore tell you if you are driven by a strict foreman, a taskmaster or a devil. Conversely, when the Jupiter fingers bend away from the middle fingers they indicate that the ego is not troubled by a conscience and can pursue its goals without guilt or moral doubt. Should you have Jupiter fingers with this outward bend you are amoral and, unless your hands show moderating features, unconcerned about little else other than your own desires and cravings.

Twisted Jupiter fingers are symbolic of an ego that is pulled this way and that, which means that if your forefingers have such a twist you probably behave selfishly and foolishly for a time which creates feelings of intense guilt and shame in you later. The cycle then repeats itself and you go off the rails again until the Furies once more bring you to heel.

Thus your life constantly moves between two extremes, with both sets of actions feeding off the other, while that moderate centre point continually passes you by and so deprives you of stability and happiness. The degree of twisting indicates the size of the oscillations, a slight twist marking small variations and a strong twist more acute ones.

It is important in this respect to compare the length and straightness of your left and right forefingers. Left forefinger defects are indicative of inherited and therefore deep-seated emotional or psychological difficulties, while right forefinger defects suggest those that have been developed or acquired. This means that a straight right forefinger of normal length represents a basically sound sense of self, even though the left forefinger may be too short or perhaps twisted. In this case the formative years provided sufficient love, support and encouragement to allow the personality to grow and rise above its inherited doubts and weaknesses, which though still a factor in the personality have been diluted and largely rendered harmless. A straight left forefinger coupled with a defective right forefinger shows that while the psychic substratum is sound the events of the early years have stunted the ego in some way. Here psychiatric or other professional help is likely to be successful in restoring confidence and psychic balance. Real treatment difficulties, however, are experienced with those who have both forefingers that are either too long or too short and perhaps bent and twisted, as they show that the inherited problem has been added to, or at least confirmed by, the person's life experiences.

These aspects of character are more fully revealed by the phalanges, whose length and thickness must now be considered and evaluated, as must the size of the joints and the shape of the fingertips.

The three phalanges of each Jupiter finger represent, as they do in all the fingers, the three separate, yet inter-related, worlds of thought and spirit, body and ambitions, and desires and cravings or, that is, the mental, practical and physical concerns of us all. When the phalanges are of equal length and thickness they show that these three worlds are normally and harmoniously developed. Inequalities of length and thickness therefore represent imbalance of some kind.

The first phalanx of the Jupiter finger symbolizes our mental concerns, our ideals and opinions, and our religious beliefs. If it is the longest of the three it indicates that there is an emphasis on the self from a mental point of view, that the ego has developed high standards and ideals as a way of aggrandizing itself. After all, there is no better way of feeling superior than by following a lofty path. A long first phalanx is thus the mark of the idealist, and if such a phalanx is set on a long finger the personality is necessarily based on a dangerous combination of arrogance and strong or superior belief, which can manifest as religious, political or racial bigotry. A thick phalanx accentuates these tendencies, while a thin phalanx modifies them.

When the second phalanx is the longest it indicates that the concerns of the self are directed towards practical or worldly ends, to the making of money and to the achievement of success. A long and thick second phalanx shows a single-minded determination to succeed in a business or commercial sense, and if such a phalanx appears in a forefinger that is too short it reveals that the person concerned will try to compensate for his or her inferiority feelings by becoming rich and famous.

If the third or basal phalanx is the longest of the three there is an emphasis on physical concerns, on the gaining of pleasure by satisfying bodily cravings for food, drink and sex. A long third phalanx, especially if it is thick, is therefore the mark of the glutton and the sensualist. Thus it comes as no surprise to find such phalanges on the hands of fat people. A thin third phalanx, however, is a sign of pulmonary weakness, particularly if it is waisted. Those with thin basal phalanges in their forefingers should avoid smoking and work that exposes them to dust or noxious fumes.

Because the fingertips are an integral part of the first or mental phalanges, their shape gives a further insight into mental functioning. There are four main fingertip shapes: pointed, conical, square and spatulate. These are illustrated in Figure 3.

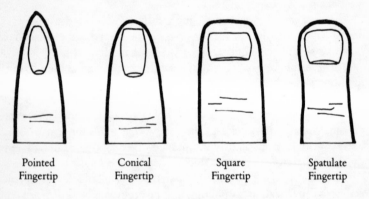

| Pointed | Conical | Square | Spatulate |
| Fingertip | Fingertip | Fingertip | Fingertip |

Figure 3

Pointed and conical fingertips symbolize intuitive or irrational qualities of mind: impracticality, sensitivity and artistic awareness. Square and spatulate fingertips are symbolic of intellectual or rational mental qualities, those of sense, practicality, confidence and order.

If the tips of your Jupiter fingers are pointed you have a very idealistic and impractical type of mind, one that will be extremely self-absorbed if the first phalanges are the longest of the three. You are the sort of person who feels separate from the world and you may well have considered cutting yourself off from it by becoming a hermit or solitary. High-flown poets and philosophers have fingertips of this type. You may have difficulty in achieving anything solid because your feet are not really in contact with the ground.

Conical fingertips represent a less elevated and fanciful mind, yet one that is still governed by instinct and feeling. If you have conical first fingertips, again especially if the phalanges are long, you are a restless, active and impulsive person. Your mood varies a lot, dependent as it is upon the circumstances in which you find yourself. You are very sensitive to colour, music and art, and quite probably your interests and ambitions centre on these.

Should your first fingertips be square in form you are an orderly, practical, loyal and rather unadventurous person. If the first phalanges are also long, you are quite certain of what you want out of life and how you are going to get it. However, you tend to resist new ideas, which can sometimes be to your disadvantage. In your interactions with others you are bluff and to the point.

The spatulate fingertip is the ideal in many ways, symbolizing as it does vitality, enthusiasm and confidence. If you have spatulate first fingertips you possess a free and open mind, which means that you are always ready to try something different. In this respect you are an adventurer and a rebel, characteristics that are accentuated if your first forefinger phalanges are also long. Thus your contribution to the world, should you be endowed with talent, is likely to be novel and inventive.

If the joints or the knuckles of your fingers are prominent you are a thorough, analytical type of person and your thoughts and interests are practical and sober. Should your first forefinger knuckles be knotted and and the second smooth, your need for order and precision is centred on on your mental life, so that you think deeply and carefully. Thus you can only be swayed by a well-reasoned argument. The progress that you make is orderly as you insist on planning ahead and sticking to the time-table. Thus while you miss out on the thrill and excitement of risk-taking, you will always be safe. A prominent second knuckle on your forefingers indicates that you dress neatly and conservatively, and that you are orderly at home and at work. Such attention to detail is enhanced if your fingers are long, but reduced if they are short. Long fingers symbolize prudence, caution and love of detail, short fingers the reverse, that is, a more impulsive and impatient attitude.

Smooth fingers or those lacking prominent knuckles are similar in meaning to short fingers, which indicates that they are representative of an intuitive and less centred mental mode. If you have smooth first fingers you are impressionable and changeable, and are blessed with a livelier and more outgoing personality than the owner of knotted first fingers. Indeed, one or more of your interests will be musical or artistic. You dislike details, but easily get caught up in the grand sweep of things. Should your first fingers be short and smooth you are a fly-by-night, an unsettled person who is easily bored and hard to please. But if your forefingers are long you are more settled and capable.

The **MEDIUS** or second finger, which is normally the longest of the four, is named after Saturn, whom the Greeks called Cronus and who came to power by emasculating his father Uranus with a flint sickle. He was in turn deposed by his son Jupiter (or Zeus), who killed him with a thunderbolt. The middle finger is traditionally called the 'fool's finger', quite probably because Saturn was fooled by his wife Rhea into believing he had eaten Zeus when he had in fact swallowed a rock. The name of the right-hand middle finger's Dactyl, Epimedes, meaning 'he who thinks too late', emphasizes this association with slow wits. The god Saturn was a Roman agricultural deity, which likewise suggests low intellect, although the Dactyl of the left-hand middle finger would certainly have had more in common with Cronus, which means 'crow', a bird once thought to have oracular powers, as the middle fingers are also linked with wisdom and divination. Indeed, the ancient Greeks looked back longingly to the golden age of Cronus, when mankind knew nothing of warfare and lived off the fruits of the land.

The middle finger has also long had sexual associations, due to its use as an arouser and frequently a satisfier of female passion. This is why it was commonly called *Digitus obscenus*, the 'dirty finger'. A raised middle finger is still used to express contempt—'Up yours'.

Standing between the thumb and forefinger, the digits of personal force and the ego, on the one side and the third and fourth fingers, those of intuition, art and sex, on the other, the middle fingers symbolize the control mechanism that lies between the conscious and the unconscious parts of the mind. Thus they represent, in Freudian terms, the super-ego, or the censor or conscience. This is why the middle fingers stand for caution, prudence and common sense, and the use of reason and the mind. Weak middle fingers therefore reveal a lack of control, while those that are very strongly formed are symbolic of a repressed psyche.

If your middle fingers are straight, well-formed and of normal length, they indicate that your conscience is adequately developed. You possess self-control, but you do not have it in excess. This indicates that you feel good about yourself and that you are neither psychologically ill-disciplined nor wracked with guilt. Such inner balance aids you in finding happiness.

However, if your middle fingers are straight but too long, to the extent that the base of their nails stand well above the ends of the index and third fingers, this reveals that both the intellectual and intuitive side of your personality are subject to strict control. This means that you are a worrier, that you have trouble relaxing and sleeping, that you are overly concerned with your health and appearance, and that you carefully channel your energies into those activities that are socially acceptable. Such preoccupation with your inner and outer self is intensely selfish, and your needs and wishes are your main concern. You are also probably rather aloof, humourless, difficult to get to know and frightened of your emotions. And when you fall sick you tend to suffer from disorders of the nervous system, intestines or the sexual organs. Lack of self-control is shown by middle fingers that are only as long as, or shorter than, the first and third fingers. If you have such fingers you are restless and impatient.

Should your middle fingers lean towards your forefingers, that is, towards the conscious half of the hand, then your repressive tendencies are focussed on the conscious part of yourself, which means that you are very correct and ordered outwardly. You therefore tend to seek constant approval and to be much concerned about how you conduct yourself. Thus your behaviour, opinions and style of dress are tailored to suit the group or social stratum that you wish to impress. In this sense you are a born politician, and indeed politics, public speaking, art, music and even sex are areas that attract you, stemming as they do from the non-repressed intuitive side of yourself. You are freer and more relaxed in private than you are in public, which indicates that you may have one or more skeletons in the cupboard. Hence you won't be surprised to learn that many people in the public eye have middle fingers of this type.

If your middle fingers lean in the opposite direction, towards the third fingers or the unconscious half of your hands, then your repressions are turned inwards. This makes you a difficult person to know intimately as you are reluctant to reveal much about yourself. If this tendency is carried too far you may limit your talk and interests to surface things, which gives you a deceptively shallow manner. Yet because your repression is directed away from your outer self, your social persona is much freer than that of the person whose middle fingers bend towards their forefingers. This is why you don't pay much attention to rules and why you dress and behave somewhat unconventionally. Unfortunately, however, your unresolved conflicts may adversely affect your attitudes and behaviour through transference.

The second fingers must also be judged by the length and thickness of their phalanges, the shape of their tips and the smoothness or knottiness of their knuckles.

If the first phalanx is the longest of the three it shows you to be an introspective person who sets high standards for yourself. You have a thoughtful, serious, but over-anxious mind, which makes you a worrier. Your anxiety is more acute if your middle fingers are long and if their first knuckle is knotted. It is less if the fingers are short and smooth.

Your hopes for yourself are rather dreamy and impractical if your second fingertips are pointed, which makes it hard for you to achieve anything solid or worthwhile. You are also scatty and illogical, and unfortunately superstitious. Conical second fingertips indicate greater common sense and a sharper wit. If you have such fingertips you are, however, quite idealistic. If your second fingertips are square you are stable and centred and have a sensible attitude to the world. Should they be spatulate in form you are able to laugh at yourself, which naturally stops you from being boring and pompous. You are also able to direct your energies into original and satisfying channels.

The second phalanx of the fingers symbolizes your attitude to the material or workaday world. Should this be the longest phalanx of your second fingers you are very much drawn towards Saturnian activities like mining, agriculture, science, oil and mineral exploration, history, antiques and languages, which means that you may work in one of these fields. More ominously, because Saturn is connected with theft and other crimes you may be light-fingered or possibly involved in shady activities. A knotted second knuckle is the mark of the specialist and of the collector—of other people's property if the phalanx is long!—while a smooth second knuckle is indicative of a more open, less materialistic mind.

The basal or third phalanx is symbolic of the lower or animal desires. If this is the longest phalanx of your second fingers you are fascinated by the seamier side of sex, to the extent that you may enjoy visiting those areas of town where there are strip clubs, massage parlours and brothels. Similarly, you enjoy reading about sex and looking at dirty pictures. Yet you are more comfortable in the role of a spectator than as a participant. Sexual perversion is evident if other negative hand features, such as abnormal little fingers, are present.

The **ANNULUS** or third finger is named after Apollo, the Lord of Light. The Dactyl of the right-hand third finger was named Iasius, which means 'healer', and indeed in former times this finger was used by apothecaries to stir and mix healing potions and powders. The third finger of the left hand was used to stir mixtures that were poisonous. Early healers were in reality witch-doctors, who could both cure and curse. This dual function is referred to in the myth of Asclepius, the son of Apollo and the traditional founder of medicine, who was given two phials of the Gorgon Medusa's blood by the goddess Athene. The blood in one, which had been taken from Medusa's right side, gave Asclepius the power to kill, while that of the other, which had been removed from the Gorgon's left side, enabled him to raise the dead. It is also of interest to note that Asclepius was taught the art of healing by the centaur Cheiron, whose name means 'hand'.

Apollo was not only the god of healing but also of the arts and prophecy, which naturally connects the third fingers with these. The ancient Greeks knew that artistic ideas and prophetic inspirations rose up from the deeper parts of the mind, so it is right for these gifts to be associated with fingers placed in the unconscious or intuitive part of the hands.

The third fingers are thus symbolic of emotional stability, artistic and intuitive sensitivity, and the health of those organs and body parts ruled by the Sun, such as the heart, blood, brain, appendix and right eye. Third finger deficiences indicate problems in these areas.

In length, the third fingers should equal that of the forefingers and both should reach to the mid-point of the first phalange of the second finger. Longer third fingers are long, shorter ones are short.

If you have third fingers that are straight, well formed and of normal length, you are blessed with stable emotions, a robust heart and cardiac system, and a friendly and outgoing or sunny disposition. Your sensitivity enables you to bring an artist's eye to how you dress, speak and behave and to how you furnish and arrange your home, which gives you style. Ideally, you want your clothes and your surroundings to suggest uplift and harmony. You are also fond of the arts and you may have one or more artistic hobbies or interests.

However, these positive characteristics are not so well developed if either the middle or the fourth fingers lean towards your third fingers, the former indicating, as we have seen, emotional repression, the latter an over-concern with sex. And while your third fingers can show if you possess artistic awareness and how your talents are expressed, they do not reveal artistic talent in itself.

Third fingers that are too long are a sign of emotional imbalance, suggesting as they do that the emotions dominate the mind. If your third fingers are longer than normal then you are a victim of your feelings, which means that you laugh, cry and hurt easily. Your emotional responses make you impulsive, so prompting you to spend money and otherwise behave without thinking. And because you find it hard to resist an appeal for help, you are an easy target for the shyster and the con-man. You are, then, too soft-hearted.

If your third fingers equal or exceed the middle fingers in length you are not simply impulsive, but rash. Additionally, your strong intuition gives you hunches and these encourage you to chance your luck and to gamble. You enjoy taking risks and you would rather win money than earn it. And because you try to achieve your goals through the use of charm, guile and persuasion, you can only succeed if luck stays with you. But luck is a fickle friend, which suggests that you will come unstuck sooner or later.

Your emotional and intuitive side is underdeveloped if your third fingers are too short, a state that may have arisen because you were emotionally deprived as a child. Thus you have a strong need for love and for being wanted, which may stop you from becoming fully mature. Your emotional needs affect your relationships because your demands frighten your partners away and this compounds your problem. And because your intuition is poorly developed you have trouble understanding yourself and others, which again works to your disadvantage. Your distorted self-image prevents you from properly estimating your talents and strengths, and thus you tend, by way of compensation, to overestimate your abilities. Hardly surprisingly, many entertainers and politicians have third fingers that are too short.

Emotional difficulties are revealed by third fingers that lean towards the middle fingers as if they were trying to shelter beneath them. This shows that the emotions are hidden behind a mask of reason. If your third fingers are of this type your emotions scare you and this has you erecting protective barriers, which is why you mistrust others and why you find it hard, if not impossible, to fall in love. It is very difficult for you therefore to have open and loving relationships. And as such third fingers bending also indicates shrewdness, you are adept at manipulating others to your own advantage.

Crooked or twisted third fingers are a sign of emotional conflict, of being twisted up inside. If your third fingers are so deformed you do not feel wholly right about yourself and your hate and anger may make you unstable and possibly violent. Crooked third fingers are also indicators of cardiac weakness, a condition that is encouraged by the inner tension and self-hate that such fingers betoken. In this respect it is important for you to have a regular health check-up, but more importantly you should get help with the emotional imbalance that is undermining your constitution and depriving you of peace of mind.

If your third fingers are smooth you are free and open emotionally and you have a good intuitive understanding of yourself, an intuitive responsiveness that is even greater if your third fingers are also long. Knotted third fingers show less emotional openness and a limited self-awareness, thus if both your third finger knuckles are prominent you have trouble in communicating both with yourself and with other people. A smooth first knuckle reveals verbal openness, but if this is combined with a knotted basal knuckle there are certain aspects of yourself that you keep secret. Because knotted knuckles symbolize a barrier to both intuitive and creative expression, you cannot have artistic talent of a high order if your third finger knuckles are large.

The phalanges of your third fingers show how you make use of your talents. If they are of equal length then you can both produce ideas and market them, which makes you an all-rounder. Hence you are well-equipped to succeed.

Should the first phalanx of your third finger be the longest your artistic mental world is the most important, which may give you the ideas but not the wherewithal to capitalize on them. This is why it is necessary for you to have a good agent. But if you lack the necessary talent to become a creative artist, your aspirations in this direction cannot be fulfilled and you may suffer much frustration and disappointment. This in turn will adversely affect your chances of finding happiness.

If the second phalanx of your third fingers is the longest one then your business instincts are good. You are competent to market your work or, if you lack creative talents yourself, the work of others. This is why managers and agents often have third fingers with a long second phalanx.

As the third or lowest phalanx relates to base desires, to sex, eating and pleasure in general, you are, if this phalanx is the longest of your third fingers, attracted to the arts not for aesthetic reasons, but because they give you access to a freer and more licentious way of life. Hence you may dress and behave ostentatiously, affecting a manner that is arty and showy.

Your talents have a visionary and impractical nature if your third fingertips are pointed, which makes you extreme and avant-garde. Should your third fingertips be conic you have a lively and expressive artistic nature, while if they are square you have more common sense and also astute money-making skills. If your third fingertips are spatulate, you possess an original and innovative mind and a talent for drama. Thus you are more likely to create or participate in artistic productions that are different in form and style.

The **QUARTERNUS** or fourth finger of the hands is named after

Mercury, or Hermes, the son of Jupiter and the nymph Maia. The Dactyl of the right-hand fourth finger was Acesidas, the 'avenger from Mount Ida', which may be a reference to Zeus or Jupiter himself. Jupiter grew to manhood on Mount Ida and was later to avenge his brothers and sisters by killing their father Saturn, who had eaten them.

In early times Mercury was a god of fertility, increase and good fortune, who was represented by a phallic pillar or *herm* that the Greeks set up outside their homes. Later, Mercury became the god of magic and intelligence—his inventions were said to have included mathematics, boxing and gymnastics, and weights and measures— and, like Apollo, of music; the musical scale, the shepherd's pipe and the tortoiseshell lyre were all attributed to him. And because cleverness originally meant an ability to lie and deceive, he was also worshipped as the god of trickery and theft. He was similarly said to possess a power over animals—his greatest feat in myth was the slaying of Argus, a hundred-eyed monster—and the gift of divination. He likewise gave protection to travellers, presided over the signing of treaties, and promoted business and commerce, which is why words such as 'merchant' and 'mercantile' derive from the same root as Mercury. He was also the messenger of the gods, the bringer of sleep and the conductor of dead souls to the underworld. Hardly surprisingly, Mercury was the busiest of the gods!

The fourth fingers symbolize sexuality and the ability or otherwise to form satisfactory sexual relationships. They also pertain to communication skills, that is, to speech and self-expression generally, business acumen, musicality and intuitive awareness.

If your fourth fingers are straight, well formed and reach to the first knuckle line of the third finger, your sexual nature is properly developed and harmoniously integrated into your personality, which implies that your sexual needs are normal and that your close relationships are happy and fulfilling. You have good intuition, which helps you understand both yourself and others, and an emotional calmness. Your inner peace contributes to your general health and suggests that you are unlikely to suffer from ailments of the bladder, kidneys and sexual organs, all of which are associated with the fourth fingers. And you also have above-average verbal and musical skills.

However, your sex drive cannot be gauged from an examination of the fourth fingers alone because it is part of your overall vital or body energy, whose quantity is symbolized by the thumbs and the mounts of Venus. A deficiency of these indicates a low sex drive, a fullness the reverse.

Ideally, the four fingers should be set levelly or in a gently curving slope on top of the palm. Yet quite often the fourth fingers are set lower than the rest, to the extent that they look as though they have taken a step down. This low setting reveals a parent fixation, which in turn brings difficulties in finding a suitable marriage partner and in forming other close relationships. Hence it is not surprising to find low-set fourth fingers on the hands of monks, nuns, hermits and other solitaries in a sexual sense, as they can, if supportive features are also present in the hands, reveal spiritual elevation and holiness. If you have low-set fourth fingers you will also find that money does not come to you easily. Indeed, should gaps be visible between your fingers when you close them together, you are unlikely to ever become rich.

Your fourth fingers are long if they extend beyond the first knuckle line of the third fingers. Because long fingers betoken caution and a love of detail, such long fourth fingers indicate that you are hesitant about entering into new sexual relationships and that you need to know your partner well before embarking on intimacy. Thus you are not promiscuous. You are also a fluent and interesting talker, and quite probably a clever and perceptive writer as well. You are polite and well-mannered, but while it takes a lot to make you lose your temper, once angered or hurt it takes a long time for you to be able to forgive.

Short fingers symbolize hastiness and impatience, so if your fourth fingers are short you are quick and impulsive in what you say and do in a sexual sense. This indicates that you are inclined to enter into new sexual relationships too quickly, which means that they are often not very long lasting, particularly as you are unable to commit yourself very deeply. Your temper is also short and rather sharp, which contributes to your relationship difficulties, although you can soon forgive and forget. You are also abusive and vulgar when you get angry as your verbal fluency is not great. Very short fourth fingers reveal a preoccupation with sex and, if other negative hand features are present, deviant sexual behaviour.

Your fourth fingers may appear to be shorter than they really are if they are low-set. This shortening of the fingers by their low setting symbolizes the negative modification that your parent fixation has had on your sexual nature. It does however indicate that with suitable psychiatric help your sexual nature could be restored to its natural expression.

Sexual difficulties are likewise evident if your fourth fingers stand apart from or lean away from your third fingers. This spacing indicates that your sexuality is not fully integrated into your personality, perhaps because you were made to feel guilty about sex as a child. You therefore tend to behave furtively where sex is concerned and this is why your sexual relationships are short and lacking in emotional content.

You are not entirely honest if your fourth fingers are twisted, especially where your feelings are concerned. Lies come easily to your lips and while you may not try to deceive in a criminal sense, it is hard for you to be straightforward and open. Twisted fourth fingers are also a mark of shrewdness and astuteness. Take note that they can sometimes indicate an under-active thyroid gland.

Knotted fourth fingers reveal an analytical brain and careful, ordered thought processes. Hence if you have fourth fingers with large knuckles you are likely to be steadfast and enterprising and to have good commercial instincts. If your fourth fingers are smooth you possess a good intuitive understanding of your sexual nature, which helps you communicate with the opposite sex, and a receptivity to music and art. Should only the first joint be knotted, your thoughts and ideas are very logical and controlled. But if the lower joints are the only ones that are prominent, then you are very fussy about your personal appearance and habits, particularly those habits of an amorous and nocturnal nature.

When the first phalanx of the fourth fingers is the longest it is a sign of verbal charm, thus you have a fluid and persuasive tongue if this is the longest phalanx of your little fingers. Should this phalanx bend towards the third fingers, your skill with words is accompanied by great tact, which necessarily makes you a natural diplomat.

If the second phalanx of your fourth fingers is the longest you have a talent for science and business. This suggests that much of your sexual energy is diverted into your work, whose demands and the tiredness it produces provides you with an excuse for not exerting yourself between the sheets.

You have strong sexual desires if the third phalanx of your fourth fingers is the longest and these will require frequent gratification if the fingers are also short and smooth. Because you are preoccupied with sex, your thoughts and interests are focussed on the salacious and the obscene.

You are irreverent and unconventional if your little fingers are pointed—about sex and most other things. Conical fingertips reveal a similar unconventionality, but one that is more centred, notably where your artistic interests are concerned. Square fourth fingertips show that your conversation is sensible, reasoned and down-to-earth. You don't like beating around the bush either. If your fourth fingers are spatulate you have an engaging and original way of expressing yourself.

The foregoing has shown that the thumbs essentially symbolize will-power; the forefingers, the ego; the middle fingers, self-control; the third fingers, intuition and emotion; and the fourth fingers, sex. We must now consider how these meanings are affected by the placement of the fingers on either the right or the left hand.

If you carefully compare the thumbs and fingers of your two hands you will soon see that they are not exactly the same. The digits of one hand, for example, may be longer or thicker or more bent than their opposites on the other. The gaps between the fingers may also be different in size.

There is nothing strange or necessarily abnormal about these differences. Rather, it would be surprising if they were not present because each hand symbolizes, as we have already noted, different aspects of ourselves. Your left hand represents your unconscious mind and your inherited mental and physical self, your right hand your conscious mind and the person you have developed into. Thus, considered together, the hands symbolize your whole self.

Simply put, this means that when you examine the thumb and fingers of your left hand you are looking at portions of your psychic and physical substratum, while when you turn your attention to your right hand you are seeing the part of your personality that has flowered on that basal earth. And this is true if you are right- or left-handed.

Let us suppose, by way of example, that the fourth finger of your left hand is straight, well formed, of normal length, set on a level with the other fingers and does not stand noticeably apart from the third finger. As we have seen, this symbolizes a normal and healthy sexuality. But if your right fourth finger shows some departure from this ideal form, by perhaps being shorter or lower-set or bent, then this shows that your sexuality has been negatively changed to some extent by your life experiences. This does not mean that you've been turned into a deviate, but that maybe you have developed an uncertainty or a lack of confidence about your sexuality that stops you from being wholly at peace with yourself.

Or your right fourth finger could have an ideal form, while your left fourth finger displays some abnormal trait. Should this be the case then your upbringing will have positively altered an inherited insufficiency in your sexual nature. Thus although your psychic substratum is flawed, you have been lucky enough to have developed a basically sound sexuality.

The character strengths that may be revealed by the left hand therefore provide a firm base on which positive change can be brought about if the developed traits shown by the right hand are deficient. Such change often happens spontaneously as part of the normal maturation process or it can be helped along with the help of professionals like psychiatrists. Change of this sort is much more difficult to bring about if the psychic bedrock is deficient or abnormal, which is why some people respond more slowly to psychiatric help than others.

This means that if you want to obtain a complete picture of yourself or of anybody else you must carefully examine and compare both hands. To look at only one of them is like trying to tell the time by a clock with only one hand.

5

THE FINGERNAILS AND
FINGERPRINT PATTERNS

We must next consider the nails and the fingerprint patterns, as both can give important insights into character and general health.

The nails are judged on their size, shape and colour, and on any unusual features that they show, such as white flecks and ribbing.

The ideal nails are in balance with the size of the hands, are smooth, shiny and strong, have visible moons and a healthy pink colour. Nails like this betoken a frank, open and cheerful personality and a robust constitution. Nails that depart from this ideal to any extent reveal deficiencies of both character and health.

Nails that are small, yet well shaped and lacking in any negative features, mark a refined character and a general sweetness of disposition, but also a lack of energy and a tendency to be fussy. Small nails that are brittle and pale in colour, or flecked with white spots, are indicative of an underlying anxiety, which turns the fussiness into prissiness, compulsion and hypochondria. Should such nails have a blue colouration they are a sign of circulatory disorders.

Large nails that are not unnaturally thick or curved, and which have a pink colour, symbolize vitality and a generous, sociable and outspoken manner. If they are red in colour then the personality is brasher and more forceful. When large, red nails accompany strong thumbs and long, thick forefingers they betoken a person who is opinionated and somewhat intimidating. Such people find it very hard to back down in an argument or to change their views.

Large nails that display negative features, especially those of curvature and colour, reveal health problems relating to the heart and circulatory system. If they are curved or bulbous and have a blue colour, they indicate cardiac abnormalities. Large nails with prominent moons are the sign of an irregular circulation. If they lack moons, and this also applies to nails of any size and shape, then the blood pressure is low and the circulation poor.

Nail shape is likewise important. Long nails are longer than their
width, short nails are shorter than their width. Fan-shaped nails are
broader at their top than at their base. Figure 4 illustrates these three
principal nail shapes.

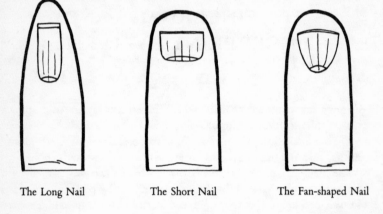

The Long Nail   The Short Nail   The Fan-shaped Nail

Figure 4

Long nails belong to the person with a quiet, easy-going manner and
who is intuitive, idealistic and artistic. Indeed, the longer the nails the
less angry is the personality. Those with long nails usually express their
annoyance as sarcasm when upset.

But where the health is concerned, long nails symbolize a weak
constitution and a predisposition to disorders of the lungs and chest,
especially if they are thin, curved, ribbed or fluted. Should such nails
have a basal bluish tinge and be white at their tops they show a tendency
to throat problems. Long nails with large moons are a sign of an over-
active thyroid gland.

Short nails are symbolic of an angry dispotition, and those who
possess them tend to be critical, argumentative and easily provoked.
They are also the mark of a logical mind. Very short nails betoken a
belligerent, explosive personality.

Like large, red and curved nails, short nails show a predisposition to
heart diseases. When thin and lacking moons, short nails reveal an actual
heart weakness. If they are white in colour then the personality is rather
cold and heartless, and the blood lacks iron. Large moons on short nails
are a positive feature, as they reveal good blood circulation. Short, brittle
and ridged nails are indicative of an improperly functioning thyroid gland.

Nails that are fan-shaped are symptomatic of anxiety and a general nervousness, which in turn points to a predisposition to psychic disorders and to diseases of the nervous system. A paralytic tendency is suggested by fan-shaped nails that are thin, short and flat.

When white flecks are visible under the nails they signify a nervous system that is stressed, and are thus indicators of worry and general unhappiness. The same applies to those who habitually bite their nails. Such people are anxious and insecure.

Less well known is the significance of the fingerprint patterns. Fingerprints are, of course, used by police forces throughout the world as a method of identifying criminals, but they are equally useful in determining traits of character.

If you look closely at the skin of your palms and fingers you will be able to see that it is covered with very fine lines running parallel to each other. These form a background to the more obvious palm and finger lines.

These skin pattern lines are known technically as the epidermal or papillary ridges. If you examine them through a magnifying glass you should be able to make out what appears to be small dots running along them. These are the openings of the sweat glands.

The epidermal ridges form distinct patterns on the fingertips, flowing together as they do into wave-like shapes or circles. There are three main types of fingerprint pattern shapes: the arch, the loop and the whorl. These are illustrated in Figure 5.

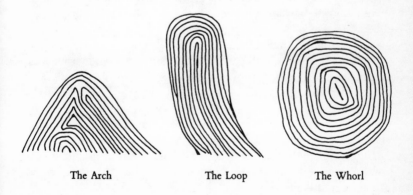

The Arch   The Loop   The Whorl

Figure 5

The arch is the simplest of the three types, the epidermal ridges forming a shape like a hump or bridge. A more complex arch form is the

tented arch, which has an upright central core around which the skin
pattern lines flow. Both types of arch are quite common.

The loop is really an elongated arch. There are two types of loop,
each of which leans in the opposite direction. The more frequently
found ulnar loop leans towards the thumb, the rarer radial loop leans
towards the little finger. Loops are usually found on one or more of the
fingers.

The whorl is circular in shape and also comes in two forms. In the
whorl type shown in the diagram the skin pattern lines are arranged in a
series of concentric circles, while in the other they lie in a spiral.

Quite often the fingerprint pattern of one finger is different from
that of the corresponding finger of the other hand. In this case that of the
right hand reveals the developed character trait or traits and that of the
left hand the latent or hidden trait or traits.

The arch fingerprint pattern is the simplest and therefore the most
primitive of the three types. It is most commonly found on the index
fingers, but seldom occurs on the ring or little fingers. When arch
patterns appear on all the fingers they are the sign of a basic and
unrefined personality whose concerns are limited and selfish. The
character has a stubborn streak and new things are regarded with
suspicion, even fear. There is also a lack of spontaneity and openness. Yet
this type of person is practical and has a liking and sometimes a talent for
the plastic arts.

An arch on the index fingers reveals a calm, practical and honest
person, who is stubborn and courageous but who finds it difficult to
discuss or even show his or her inner feelings. Such people have a love of
the past and of tradition.

The person with arch patterns on the middle fingers is cautious, hard-
working and religious, and is drawn to the land and to outdoor pursuits.
He or she likes solitude, yet has a tendency towards depression. And
while others are dealt with fairly and honestly, the concerns are self-
centred.

When present on the third fingers the arch indicates that the creative
energies are directed towards practical ends. Because there is also a love
of natural materials like clay, wood and stone, those with third-finger
arch patterns often work in occupations where these are used, such as
carpentry and building.

It is rare to find an arch pattern on the fourth fingers. When present it
is the mark of a selfish person whose passions are strong and whose
sexual nature is direct and earthy.

The tented arch is similarly found most frequently on the index
fingers, where it symbolizes greater sensitivity than the simple arch. If it

occurs on the middle fingers it reveals a person who enjoys being part of a group, especially one that has a cause or mission. Musical and artistic talents are indicated when this pattern is located on the third fingers, and a warm, passionate but complex sexuality when it is found on the fourth fingers.

An arch on the thumbs represents strong will-power and as such adds to that revealed by large, thick thumbs. A tented arch on the thumbs shows that the will-power is adaptable.

The loop is the most common fingerprint pattern. Of the two types described, the ulnar loop, which leans towards the thumbs, is more frequently seen than the radial loop. When present, the latter invariably occurs on the third fingers. And because the radial loop has a very similar meaning to that of the whorl, it can be interpreted as this pattern.

Just as the arch symbolizes caution, practicality and repression, so the loop represents openness, versatility and freedom. It gives a fluid and receptive expression to the mental and emotional nature.

A loop on the index fingers indicates unselfishness and co-operativeness. The character is less uptight and jealous than that of those who have arch or whorl patterns on this finger. And because it represents flexibility, those who have loops on their first fingers are able to change course when obstacles are encountered.

A loop on the middle fingers represents an optimistic and generally cheerful nature and an open mind. If high-set, the loop shows a talent for scientific research. If low-set, it indicates a love of the outdoors and of country pursuits.

When a loop is present on the third fingers it is a sign that its owner is sensitive to beauty and receptive to fresh artistic ideas. A high-set loop shows an interest in pure art, a low-set loop a preference for fashion, design and decoration.

On the fourth fingers a loop indicates friendliness, a sense of humour, good speaking skills and a normal sex urge.

And when it is found on the thumbs the loop reveals that the will is easily and vigorously expressed.

The whorl is the most complex and thus the most advanced of the three finger-pattern types. It is a very individual sign and is possessed by those who are very sure of themselves and their ideas. When it is found on several fingers it betokens someone who is so independent that he or she pays scant attention to the wishes or needs of others. It is also the mark of a secretive and somewhat tense personality.

A whorl on the first fingers symbolizes the true individual, the person who has to do things his or her way. In extreme cases this attitude becomes eccentricity. Those with this pattern carve out their own careers and are motivated by making their mark on the world. There is often, however, a tendency to specialize in one field of endeavour.

A whorl on the second fingers reveals distinctive beliefs and a strong personal philosophy, which once formulated is rigorously held to and championed. The views are unorthodox, notably those pertaining to religion. There is a talent for research, which is conducted on very individualistic and idiosyncratic lines, and a strong need to collect old and valued objects.

The third fingers are the most common site for whorls, where they indicate a very individual taste in art. It is important for those with such whorls that their creative urges are allowed free expression, as any form of restriction in this area is keenly resented. The tastes in clothing, home decoration and furnishings, cars and so on are distinctive. Indeed, this type of person loves to dare and shock others.

Whorls are seldom found on the fourth fingers. When present they indicate strongly individual ways of conducting personal relationships. There may even be unusual sexual needs. The attitude towards sex is free and open, and therefore often irresponsible. Fourth finger whorls also reveal good powers of self-expression and a sharp, though individualistic, business sense.

On the thumbs the whorl adds to their strength, yet suggests inflexibility. Those with whorls on their thumbs like to dominate others and thus find it hard to compromise.

Perhaps more interestingly, the number of loops and whorls on the fingers can give a quick insight into your fate. You can obviously have no loops at all or as many as ten, and the same applies to the number of whorls. Quite possibly your fingers have both loops and whorls. If so, count the number of each and combine their meanings as outlined below.

You are blessed if your fingers have only one loop, as this shows that you will rise to the top of your profession and acquire both wealth and power. If you have two loops you will also become wealthy, although you won't attain the same status as the owner of one loop. Three loops indicate that you have an elevated spiritual nature, which means that your religion is important to you. Indeed, should you devote your life to spiritual work or to religious study you will gain wide recognition and much affection. Four loops is an unlucky number to have, as they indicate that your life will be one of struggle, toil and hardship. If you possess five loops you are lucky with money and will become wealthy. Six loops show that you have a warm, loving nature, which gives you riches of the spirit but not of the pocket. Seven loops indicate that money is not attracted to you and that you therefore cannot become rich. Eight loops, however, are a sign that you will become wealthy. Nine loops is also an unfortunate number to have where money is concerned, although you will have success in human and spiritual terms. The possession of ten loops condemns you to a life of bad luck and poverty.

Should your fingers have but one whorl you are intelligent and resourceful. If other features of the hand are supportive, you will do well for yourself through your own efforts. Two whorls show you to be intelligent and charming, which gives you success with the opposite sex. If you have three whorls you will lead an easy, comfortable life. Four whorls make you unlucky with money and reveal that you will have a hard life. Five whorls indicate that you are an intellectual and that you will have success in your studies and in examinations. Six whorls take you one step further, as they suggest that you will lead the life of an academic. Should you have seven whorls you are a loner, thus you may shun society and become a recluse. If you have eight whorls your life will be difficult and financially troubled. Nine whorls are a wonderful sign. Should you have this number you will reach the top of your profession and achieve much honour and recognition. And if you have ten whorls you will lead a moderately happy and comfortable life. Thus you may become a civil servant.

6

THE WEARING OF RINGS

Before we further consider the thumbs and fingers as indicators of fate, it is necessary to examine the wearing of rings, for rings are not, as is often assumed, mere decorative additions to the hands, but have, as does so much else of what we wear, a psychological meaning.

When we buy a ring we choose one that we like and can afford—and also the finger upon which it is to be worn. It is the third choice that is important because while the first two are consciously made, the last is directed by hidden needs. This is why a ring feels mysteriously right on the finger we select, but quite wrong on the others.

But what does a ring do for the finger it graces? The answer is simple: it augments the finger and thus draws attention to it. And by making the finger stand out we are unconsciously making a reference to those aspects of ourselves that the finger represents. We do this because those character traits are not properly integrated into our psyche, and this causes us discomfort and anxiety. The ring expresses our disquiet and so acts as a warning to others, while at the same time asking for understanding.

But there are rings and rings. Some are little more than thin bands, some are modestly adorned with one or two stones, and some are thick circles of metal encrusted with diamonds or other precious gems. An expensive ring naturally tells the world that its wearer is rich or has a wealthy husband or admirer, but a big ring is a clear sign of personality difficulties. It is, quite simply, a question of size. Small rings speak softly, large ones shout. And the louder the shout, the larger is the problem.

The size of the ring must be related to the length of the finger on which it is worn. In practice it will be found that those with fingers of normal length, which are neither bent, twisted nor otherwise abnormal, seldom wear rings, with the exception of those worn to satisfy convention, such as engagement or wedding rings. Rings typically appear on fingers that are longer or shorter than normal, or which display some unusual bend, twist or kink. These abnormalities symbolize the problems of the ring wearer, the ring itself the disquiet that he or she experiences.

Rings worn on the left-hand fingers refer to the unsettling effects of inherited personality disorders. Those of the right hand to the anxiety caused by developed or consciously expressed personality problems.

Consider, for example, the forefingers, which represent the self or ego. If both forefingers are short this betokens an inferiority complex, but if one or both are ringed this shows that their owner feels his inferiority acutely and that he needs to actively compensate for it in some way. A ring worn on a short left forefinger says that this is being done inwardly by eating or drinking excessively or through educational over-achievement, while a ring on a short right forefinger reveals that aggrandizement is sought by dominating others. The latter ring is therefore the badge of the petty tyrant.

However, when someone with long forefingers wears rings on them it suggests that he is troubled by his overbearing manner and is trying to find excuses for it. A ring worn on the long left forefinger shows that the blame is turned inwardly and that the person concerned is self-deprecating. A ring on a long right forefinger reveals that blame is placed on the outside world, which necessarily marks the wearer out as a chronic complainer.

Clearly then, when rings are worn on both forefingers, whether these be long or short, it indicates that the anxiety is directed inwardly and outwardly. This makes the wearer doubly troubled.

Long middle or Saturn fingers are symbolic of a personality that is held under tight control by the inner censor. A ring worn on a long left middle finger acts as an extra knuckle, which in turn suggests that the repressed energies are being held down more tightly, perhaps because they are, like the Cyclopes that Saturn confined to Tartarus, struggling to be free. Such a ring therefore indicates guilt and inner turmoil and, as a consequence, considerable unhappiness. A ring worn on a long right middle finger shows that its wearer is attempting to impose his inner rigidity on the world around him. Hence it represents the critic and the carper, the person who is holier-than-thou and, very often, the political extremist who believes that he has all the answers to the world's problems.

Short middle fingers betray a conscience that is underdeveloped and hence the person who lacks self control. Rings worn on these fingers show the development, albeit in embryo form, of a conscience, as they serve as warnings to others of the instability of the character. Such control is only functioning at a lower or unconscious level if the ring is worn on a short left middle finger, but is consciously expressed if it is worn on a short right middle finger.

The third or Apollo fingers are the commonest sites for rings, which is not surprising in view of the fact that they symbolize our emotional and intuitive nature. Emotions that are out of balance are revealed by third fingers that are too long or too short, or by some other abnormal feature, while the presence of a ring shows that the imbalance is causing inner disquiet. However, the evaluation of the ring or rings worn on the left Apollo finger is made more difficult because it is the traditional site for engagement and wedding rings. In this case you must be guided by the size and the number of the rings. Some women, for example, wear only their wedding ring, others both their engagement and wedding rings. But the wearing of a third ring, or an engagement or wedding ring that is unusually large, suggests that emotional difficulties relating to the marriage are being experienced at an unconscious level. This indicates that the wife is not entirely happy with her marriage, perhaps because its demands prevent her from fulfilling herself artistically and creatively. And because such disquiet is sensed but is not consciously understood it may cause irritability, difficulty in sleeping, menstrual disorders and the like.

More telling is the ring worn on the right Apollo finger, particularly if it is straight and of normal length. Such a finger symbolizes emotional stability, yet the ring shows that the artistic impulses are being frustrated, perhaps by the marriage or by other life pressures, or by simple lack of opportunity. The dammed up energies may therefore be directed to the self or to the home and garden, or to the education of the children, through whom the parent hopes to realize his or her unfulfilled dreams.

As we have seen, third fingers that are too short are a sign of emotional immaturity and of an incompletely developed intuitive sense. Hence a ring worn on a short left third finger reveals that the need for love and assurance is deeply felt, thereby producing a cloying and dependent disposition and attention-seeking behaviour. When worn on a short right third finger, the ring represents a developed guilt about the emotional imbalance that the finger symbolizes. Those with short third fingers often believe that they are cleverer and more talented than they actually are, which makes them vain and supercilious, thus a ring worn on a short right third finger is a positive sign, indicating as it does that its wearer is doing his best to master the troubling delusions.

Third fingers that are too long symbolize an excess of emotion and intuition, which means that the logical mental processes are subservient to the feelings. A ring worn on a long left third finger indicates that these inner pressures are not only making the person concerned a victim of his emotions, but are troubling him by their changeability and by their insistence. He therefore needs help in calming his inner turmoil. A ring worn on a long right third finger shows that the disquiet is caused by the excessive behaviour that this turmoil produces, such as compulsive gambling and risk-taking. The wearer knows that his actions are wrong and damaging, and is doing his best to limit them. He is thus asking for sympathy and understanding.

Fourth or Mercury finger rings relate to relationship or sexual difficulties, which is why such rings are commonly worn by lesbians and homosexuals. A ring worn on the left fourth finger shows that the sexual problems are causing inner disquiet, while a right fourth finger ring reveals that the sexual behaviour the difficulty creates is troubling the wearer. Should the fourth fingers be low-set, they indicate that the sexual difficulties derive from the parental fixation that the fingers represent. In this case the frustrated sexual energies are often directed into some compensatory activity, which is typically accumulative in character and which is pursued at the expense of normal intimacy. This explains why many businessmen and entertainers often wear rings on their right fourth fingers.

It is very unusual to see a ring worn on one or other of the thumbs. The thumbs, being the digits of Venus, are a synonym for the phallus, which is why thumb rings also have a clear sexual meaning. A ring worn on the left thumb reveals inner disquiet about the sex act, while a ring worn on the right thumb often indicates actual dissatisfaction with the sex act, which may be due to frigidity or impotence. In this respect it is interesting to note that the Greeks and Romans wore iron rings on their thumbs to restore potency.

7

FORTUNE AND THE FINGERS

Lastly, where the fingers are concerned, we must consider a little known, but most accurate and useful, method of prediction which is based on the phalanges of the fingers.

To understand how this works we must remind ourselves that the forefingers are traditionally linked with the Spring Equinox, the middle fingers with the Summer Solstice, the third fingers with the Autumn Equinox and the fourth fingers with the Winter Solstice. Hence the four fingers of each hand respectively represent the seasons of spring, summer, autumn and winter, and thus the passage of one year.

The astrological year starts on 21 March, the first day of spring, when the sun enters the zodiac sign of Aries, the Ram. When the Sun has passed through Aries and the two following signs of Taurus and Gemini, it moves into Cancer on 22 June, the Summer Solstice. The three spring signs are therefore symbolized by the three phalanges of the forefingers, Aries being identified with the first or nail phalanx, Taurus with the second or middle phalanx and Gemini with the third or basal phalanx. In a similar way the three summer signs of Cancer, Leo and Virgo are represented by the same three phalanges of the middle fingers; the three autumn signs of Libra, Scorpio and Sagittarius by the same three phalanges of the third fingers; and the three winter signs of Capricorn, Aquarius and Pisces by the phalanges of the fourth fingers. These correspondences are shown in Figure 6.

The phalanges of the thumbs, the digits of Venus, are not linked with any of the zodiac signs. Rather, the thumbs symbolize the divine force that animates and activates the world in any year. But the nature of Venus, as we have already discovered, is both positive and negative, for she is the goddess of love and the Lady of Battles, and in this respect she is identical to the two motive forces postulated by Empedocles, namely love and strife. Love, said the ancient philosopher, draws things together creatively and procreatively, while strife pushes them apart and causes

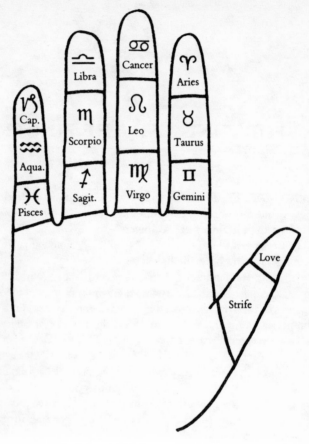

Figure 6

disharmony. The influence of these two forces produces our world of change and flux, wherein paradoxically everything is constantly changing yet remaining essentially the same.

Considered by themselves, the right thumb symbolizes love, for this is the thumb of our most useful hand, and the left thumb strife, the left hand being the one that we are least able to manipulate. But because both hands can open and close, love and strife necessarily reside in both thumbs. Strife causes the hands to open, the fingers moving away from the thumbs and each other, and love causes them to close, the fingers moving towards each other and the thumbs. In fact love is identified with the thumbs' first phalanx, that of will, and strife with the second phalanx, that of logic.

To use this predictive system you must first determine your zodiac sign of birth. Most people nowadays know their birth sign, but if you don't you can easily discover what it is by referring to the horoscope column in your daily newspaper.

Let us imagine, by way of example, that you were born on 10 August, which makes you a Leo native.

The next step is to see which phalanx of your *right hand* represents your birth sign. Figure 6 shows us that for Leo this is the middle phalanx of the middle finger.

This phalanx symbolizes your first year of life, the first knuckle line representing your birth and the lower or second knuckle line your first birthday (See Figure 7).

MIDDLE FINGER

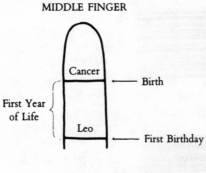

Figure 7

Should you, however, be a Pisces native then the phalanx symbolizing your first year would be the third one on your right fourth finger, if a Scorpio native it would be the middle phalanx of your right third finger, and so on.

Because each phalanx stands for one year as well as a different zodiac sign, your second year of life, again taking you as a Leo subject, is represented by the third or basal phalanx of your right middle finger (the sign of Virgo following Leo in the zodiac), which begins on your first birthday and continues until your second. The next three years are thus respectively symbolized by the three phalanges of your right third finger (counting down from the first or nail phalanx), and the following three by the phalanges of your right little finger. This means that the third phalanx of the fourth finger represents your life between its seventh and eighth birthdays.

The sequence is continued by moving to your *left-hand* index finger. The tip of this, like the lowermost knuckle line of your right-hand little finger, marks your eighth birthday. The years now follow on, going down the first finger, then down the second, third and fourth fingers, to add a further twelve years to your age, to take you to your twentieth birthday, which is symbolized by the lowermost knuckle line of your left fourth finger.

Then go back to your right hand and continue the sequence from the tip of its forefinger, to in turn add another twelve years to your life, which takes you through to your thirty-second birthday. By then moving to your left hand again you can go forward to your forty-fourth birthday, and by continuing as before you can go as far forward in time as you wish.

This means that, if you as a Leo subject are now twenty-five years old, your present state of life is symbolized by the third phalanx of the middle fingers of your right hand. By counting ahead from there you can look into the future, by counting back you can return to the past.

The quality of any year is determined by the appearance of the phalanx which symbolizes it. Ideally, the phalanx under consideration should be part of a straight finger of normal length, have a good colour, be neither too thick nor too thin, and be free of any local skin thickening, other than that produced by normal work and play activities. Such a phalanx represents a generally healthy, happy and positive year.

A year that is more successful and progressive, wherein you can achieve certain of your ambitions and goals, is shown by a phalanx that has lines running down it, which quite naturally represent the flow of the year. These lines should be straight, clearly marked, unbroken and uncrossed by other lines. The more lines of this sort that there are the better the year will be.

But when a phalanx has lines that either slope across it or, worse still, run across it at right angles to the vertical lines, perhaps to stop some of them, then it betokens a year that will be less successful and possibly quite difficult. Indeed, each transverse line represents a setback of some sort, the most troublesome of which are symbolized by lines crossing the front of the phalanx, those that cause less bother by the lines lying to the side of the phalanx. Sloping lines refer to impediments and annoyances rather than to major disappointments and problems. Figure 8 illustrates these phalanx lines.

Because each phalanx symbolizes one year, we can easily date the setbacks represented by the transverse lines. A line lying one third of the way down a phalanx marks a difficulty occurring four months after your birthday, while a line placed halfway down the phalanx stands for a negative event happening six months later, etc.

The first phalanges are usually less lined than the others. Vertical lines

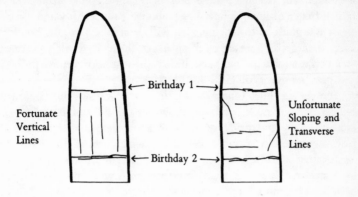

Fortunate
Vertical
Lines

← Birthday 1 →

← Birthday 2 →

Unfortunate
Sloping and
Transverse
Lines

Figure 8

are invariably absent, as are, although not so commonly, transverse lines. When the first phalanges show no lines they indicate pleasant, problem-free years, but these will not be years when much headway in a material sense can be achieved.

Moles are also sometimes present on one or more of the phalanges. If so, they are negative in meaning and therefore warn of trouble ahead. However, this only applies to moles found on the front or palmar surface of the phalanges, not to those appearing on the back of the fingers.

Moles are judged on their size, shape and colour. Small, round and light-coloured moles represent less difficult or threatening events than those symbolized by moles that are large, irregular in shape and dark in colour.

A light-coloured mole is a sign that you will suffer through your own lack of action at the time that the mole indicates. The effect of such tardiness on you is greater if the mole lies close to the mid-line of the phalanx or if it is large and irregular in outline.

Dark moles, particularly if they are large and misshapen, represent problems in your life that stem from the deceit or dishonesty of others. Their magnitude can be judged by the size and shape of the mole and by its proximity to the mid-line of the phalanx.

Ill health is symbolized by local thickenings or nodules in the skin of the phalanges, which can be caused by specific disease conditions like diabetes. When present they mark either the onset of a disease or an upsurge in its virulence. The timing of such a bad health patch can be determined by the nodule's placement, in the same manner as described for the transverse lines.

The vertical lines appearing on certain phalanges have quite specific meanings. For example, those present on the middle phalanx of the fourth finger of your right hand symbolize your fertility and can thus serve as a guide as to whether you will be childless or not. The more vertical lines that there are on this phalanx, the more fertile you are, and vice versa. Similarly, transverse lines represent both fertility problems and possible gynaecological disorders.

The vertical lines found on the third or lowermost phalanx of the fingers of your right hand are known as the lines of friendship and indicate your popularity. If several lines are present on each phalanx you have an attractive, sociable personality which attracts to you a wide circle of friends. The friendship lines should be unbroken and uncrossed by transverse lines, as such interruptions signify problems arising between you and your friends.

The number and sex of your children can be determined from your thumbs. Look at the lowest crease line of your thumbs and see if they bear islands, where they have split apart and then rejoined. Islands in the line half-circling your right thumb represent your natural children, the larger ones indicating boys, the smaller ones girls. Islands in your left thumb line signify children that will come into your life either through adoption or marriage. The order and timing of the births of your own sons and daughters can be determined by the placement of the large and

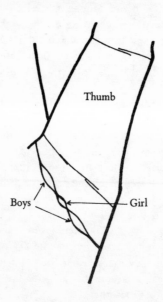

Figure 9

small islands in the right thumb line. A lower large island followed by a small one and then another large one naturally represents the birth of a boy first, followed by a girl and then another boy, giving a total of three children. The lower down on the line that the islands appear, the earlier the births. These thumb line islands are illustrated in Figure 9.

An island may also be present in the knuckle line lying between the first and second phalanges of your thumbs. Ideally, this should be clearly formed, large and centrally placed, as shown by Figure 10.

If you possess one such island you can be very glad as it is a most fortunate sign. It indicates that you will lead a happy life, find success intellectually or educationally, make money and be a credit to your family and country. Thus you can rest assured that even though things might not be going entirely well for you now, you will sooner or later do very well for yourself.

It makes no difference to your fate if the island is present on either your left thumb or your right thumb, as both are equally good. However, should both your thumbs show this island then you can consider yourself doubly blessed.

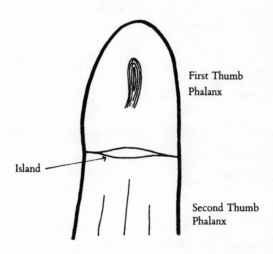

First Thumb
Phalanx

Island ——

Second Thumb
Phalanx

Figure 10

8

THE MOUNTS

We noted in the first chapter that the palms are divided into a number of distinct areas, each of which is named after one or other of the seven planets of traditional astrology. Because these areas are usually raised up somewhat above the surrounding palm surface they are known as mounts. Figure 1 shows that the mounts are arranged around the centrally-placed Plain or Triangle of Mars, the four mounts of Jupiter, Saturn, Apollo and Mercury lying below the fingers which share their names, the large Venus and Moon mounts forming the two halves of the lower palm, and that the two mounts of Mars, the mount of Lower Mars and the mount of Upper Mars, lie respectively between the mount of Venus and the mount of Jupiter on the one side and the mount of the Moon and the mount of Mercury on the other.

Because the mounts reveal much about your strengths and weaknesses, talents and tendencies, it is suggested that you examine your own hands and descry their position, size and colour for yourself.

The Mounts of Venus
The mounts of Venus are easy to find because they form the base or balls of the thumbs. Not only are they the largest mounts in area but they are also the most prominent, due to the fact that they are underlain by the muscles which move the thumbs. Their inner border is formed by the radial longitudinal line or Life line, which curves around them. You may also possess a line that runs in a sloping course from the side of the hand towards the Life line, named the *Via Mater* in Figure 11, and which, if present, symbolizes a strong attachment to your mother. This line marks the boundary between the mount of Venus and the mount of Lower Mars.

Ideally, both of your mounts of Venus should be well rounded, firm without being hard, and healthily pink in colour. They should likewise be broad, extending to about the middle of the palm, and not hemmed in

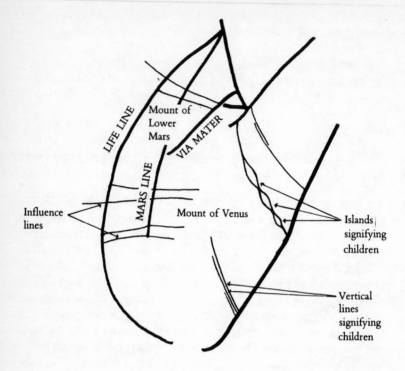

Figure 11

and made narrow by a vertically descending Life line. It is not a good sign if the Venus mounts are flat or underdeveloped or unnaturally large or overdeveloped, or if they are too soft or colourless. In this respect it is important to look for any differences in size, consistency and colour between your left and right Venus mounts, as these reflect inner imbalances.

The mounts of Venus are the prime indicators of physical vitality, and it is this that forms the foundation of good health and a happy outgoing disposition. Well-developed Venus mounts thus indicate that your digestive processes are functioning normally and that all those enzymatic and chemical reactions relating to the digestion, absorption, storage and usage of your food are working at their optimal rates. Such inner efficiency produces their pink colour, as redness is a sign of metabolic over-activity and whiteness of under-activity.

In a similar way, well-developed Venus mounts betoken an active libido (which is specifically shown by the left mount) and a healthy sex drive and full potency (which are shown by the right mount).

Deficiencies of one or both mounts reveal a disrupted energy flow and therefore a lower vitality and a weaker sex drive. Both mounts should, of course, be equally well developed.

Where the character is concerned well-rounded and pink-coloured Venus mounts are symbolic of a rising spirit, warm-heartedness, self-confidence and a friendly, happy disposition. If you have Venus mounts like this you are generous, co-operative and loving. You also like music, singing and dancing, and the pleasures of the bed.

Overdeveloped mounts of Venus signify a basic selfishness and a corresponding tendency towards excess, which derive from an improperly functioning metabolism. Should you possess large Venus mounts you probably eat and drink too much and are overly fond of sensual, particularly sexual, pleasures. You are thus at best the party type and at worst the rake or libertine.

When the mounts of Venus are flat they indicate digestive or metabolic problems and hence an inadequate supply of energy. The energy levels are lower if the mounts are also narrow, hard and white in colour. Such lack of energy robs the character of vitality and warmth, and signifies a reduced resistance to disease and a weak sex drive. If you have Venus mounts of this type you find it hard to enjoy life and you have little love for your fellow man. You are a pessimist at heart.

The lines appearing on the mounts of Venus must also be evaluated. The *Via Mater* has already been identified and when present it symbolizes a strong maternal influence. If it accompanies low-set fourth fingers the two together signify a mother fixation.

In general, the lines on the palm mounts run either vertically or horizontally. The vertical lines are positive in nature and so enhance the good qualities of the mounts. Vertical lines on the Venus mounts represent added robustness and vitality, and in this sense greatly improve Venus mounts that are flat or otherwise deficient. Horizontal lines are negative in meaning and their presence impairs the mounts. Those horizontal lines of the Venus mounts which extend to the Life line or beyond are known as the Influence lines and they symbolize psychological pressures and anxieties that may undermine the health. Indeed, when the Life line is cut by or, at worst, broken by an Influence line this signifies a health setback of some seriousness. Quite often both vertical and horizontal lines are found on the Venus mounts, which cross each other to form a grid. Such a formation is intermediate in meaning between that symbolized by either vertical lines or horizontal lines appearing on their own.

Sometimes Influence lines are seen rising from the *Via Mater* which travel to the Life line or even cross it. Each represents a period of strong

maternal influence which is sufficiently intense to affect the health or
the progress of the person concerned. However, these lines often do not
symbolize direct intervention by the mother, but mental obstacles
imposed by her conditioning.

Finally, it is worth mentioning the Hindu belief that says the vertical
lines rising from the lower edge of the Venus mounts represent children.
The longer, thicker lines symbolize boys, the shorter, thinner lines girls.

The Mounts of the Moon

The mount of the Moon or Luna lies next to the mount of Venus on each
hand, the two touching at the lower mid-line of the palm, and occupies
the bottom inner quarter of the hand. At the top of the mount is found
the mount of Upper Mars, which extends to the upper transverse line or
Heart line. There is seldom, however, any clearly marked border
between the two, the mount of Luna merging imperceptibly into the
mount of Upper Mars. The position of the Moon mount and its various
lines are shown in Figure 12.

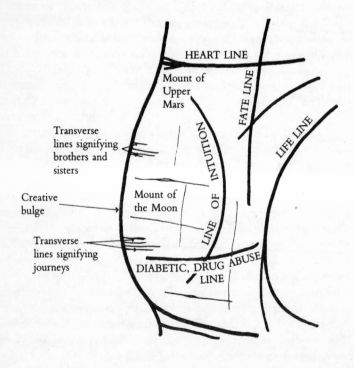

Figure 12

The mounts of the Moon should be gently curved, firm but not hard to the touch and, like the mounts of Venus, pink in colour. Yet they should not match the Venus mounts in prominence, unless of course the latter are underdeveloped. Prominent Moon mounts are overdeveloped and are therefore, like flat, hard or white Moon mounts, negative in meaning.

Just as the mounts of Venus symbolize your physical and sexual vitality, so your Luna mounts represent your degree of mental alertness and hence your imaginative and intuitive, and thus creative, powers. When they are normally developed and show no cross lines or other negative features, they signify a quiescent and untroubled mentality, yet one that is active imaginatively and intuitively. If your Moon mounts bulge outwards from the side of your hands this shows that you are sufficiently well-endowed with these latter abilities to be creative, especially artistically.

Overdeveloped mounts of the Moon symbolize a less stable psychic substratum, which produces consciously-felt anxiety, unease and a too-active imagination. Very full Luna mounts can thus be a sign of mental disorder. If you have prominent Moon mounts you are restless and flighty, abnormally sensitive and possibly depressive. When large Moon mounts are red in colour they indicate dipsomaniacal tendences, while those that are white and soft signify a predisposition to drug abuse. Flat Moon mounts are the mark of a weak intuitive sense and a lack of imagination. If such mounts are also hard and white they reveal the complete absence of imagination and intuition, which in turn indicates a pessimistic outlook and a warped view of life and human nature.

Vertical lines found on the Moon mounts enhance their imaginative and intuitive qualities. Yet they must be judged with regard to the size of the mounts, as if the Moon mounts are overdeveloped, vertical lines symbolize an excess of imagination and intuition. But the long, curving line of Intuition is of special interest. This begins low down on the Moon mounts and proceeds upwards to the mounts of Upper Mars. Because it signifies the possession of marked psychic powers, you may have telepathic, clairvoyant or precognitive abilities if the line of Intuition is clearly etched on your Luna mounts.

Cross lines on the mounts of the Moon are symbolic of both mental instability and an increased likelihood of suffering from certain physical complaints. Where the latter are concerned, the lines appearing on the top third of the mounts signify intestinal problems; those on the middle third, rheumatic disorders; and those on the bottom third, bladder, kidney and gynaecological weaknesses. The transverse lines of the left Moon mount represent a predisposition for ailments of the part or parts indicated and those of the right Moon mount suggest an incipient or active disease state. Additionally, when a long and well marked line runs across the bottom of the Moon mounts to join either the Life line cr the Fate line, this signifies diabetes.

Transverse lines that run a short way into the Moon mounts from their upper sides symbolize your brothers and sisters, the longer and broader ones representing brothers, the shorter and narrower ones sisters. Short transverse lines appearing on the side of the lower part of the Moon mounts indicate overseas journeys. When several are found they naturally suggest a restless personality.

The Mounts of Mars
The middle portion of the palm is ruled by Mars. Indeed, the palm lines that cross this area form the initial M. As we have already discovered there are two mounts of Mars, the mount of Lower Mars, so-called because it lies beneath the Life line, and the mount of Upper Mars, which are separated from one another by the centrally-placed Plain or Triangle of Mars.

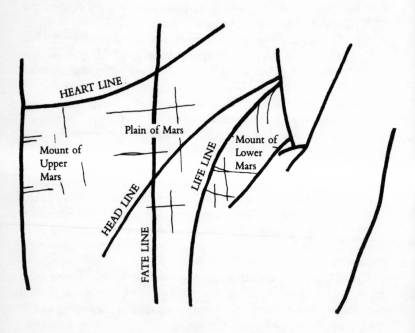

Figure 13

Together these three Mars-ruled areas reveal how much grit and spunk you have, the qualities that are so important in enabling you to fight for what you want or believe in and to resist and overcome the adversities of life.

The mounts of Lower Mars denote drive. They should be sufficiently rounded to form distinct prominences atop the mounts of Venus, and be firm to the touch and pink in colour. Such normally developed Lower Mars mounts show enthusiasm, purpose and a desire to succeed. If your Lower Mars mounts are like this you possess an innate optimism and an independent spirit, and a feeling that you are, at least to a certain extent, the master of your fate.

Overdeveloped mounts of Lower Mars are rounder and harder, their colour more red than pink. They symbolize a character full of fire and fury, thus one who is direct and forceful in getting what he wants and who will, if need be, ride roughshod over the rights of others. Hence prominent Lower Mars mounts represent selfishness and, when linked with a Plain of Mars bearing transverse lines or other defects, an ugly and possibly violent disposition. People of this type enjoy eating, drinking, fighting and copulating.

Flat mounts of Lower Mars signify, as might be expected, a lack of resolution and drive, and thus the person who is uncertain, withdrawn and lacking in confidence, the wimp. It is very hard for those with deficient mounts of Lower Mars to succeed in life as they have difficulty motivating themselves.

The qualities of character symbolized by the mounts of Upper Mars complement those of the Lower Mars mounts, standing as they do for the fuel that keeps the fire of enthusiasm going. Hence they signify the amount of persistence that you have. Few things worth having can be gained easily, which means that only those with sufficient resolve can attain their goals. Such people are those with well-developed mounts of Upper Mars and, of course, similarly developed mounts of Lower Mars.

The mounts of Upper Mars are not usually as clearly defined as are most of the other mounts, there being no distinct border between them and the lower Moon mounts and the flanking Plain of Mars. However, the area they occupy should be rounded, firm to the touch and pink in colour. When so formed, they betoken the positive qualities outlined above.

If the mounts of Upper Mars are prominently developed they are a mark of unnatural stubborness, like that of the bulldog who refuses to let go of what he has seized. Such persistence is a failing because it implies an inability to compromise or to admit that one might be wrong. Those with overdeveloped mounts of Upper Mars may spend their lives chasing the unattainable.

Flat Upper Mars mounts signify a lack of persistence and thus the person who gives up too easily. However, such mounts must be related to the thumbs, which symbolize will-power.

Both Mars mounts are strengthened by one or more vertical lines and weakened by transverse lines or grids. Transverse lines on the mounts of Upper Mars, particularly if these bear islands or a star, indicate a predisposition to ailments of the head and throat, the genitals, the rectum and the anus.

The mounts of Mars should ideally be equally well developed on both your left and right hands. If the left-hand Mars mounts are normally developed but one or both of the right-hand Mars mounts are deficient, this means that your body energies have been repressed or bottled-up by factors encountered during your development. The reverse situation is rarely encountered because it is almost impossible to acquire drive and dash if you were not born with them.

The Plains or Triangles of Mars symbolize what can be called spirit, and they thereby denote how quickly your passions can be aroused. Because the Plains of Mars are not mounts they do not show any roundness, hence in their ideal development they are flat, firm and pink in colour, revealing a sound temper and an optimistic outlook on life. Transverse lines on them betoken irrascibility, and when partnered by prominent mounts of Lower Mars signify the person who is inherently bad-tempered. If both Plains of Mars are hollow the character lacks spark and sparkle, and so has difficulty in making its presence felt. This is probably why hollow palms are said to be unlucky. Their owners are stymied by their absence of spirit.

The Apices

The four remaining palm mounts, namely those of Jupiter, Saturn, Apollo and Mercury, each lie directly under the finger that shares its name. If you examine the skin pattern lines or epidermal ridges of these mounts you will be able to see that at one point on them they run together to form triangular-shaped confluences or apices. The typical appearance of such an apex is shown in Figure 14.

Each apex marks the mount's true centre and their position should be carefully noted. Ideally, they should lie on the mid-line of the finger above them. They may, however, be displaced to one side or the other. Their setting should also be considered, as they may be centrally-set, high-set or low-set. If you place an ink dot at the centre of each mount apex you will be able to compare their placements very easily.

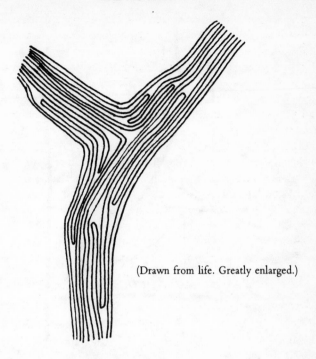

(Drawn from life. Greatly enlarged.)

Figure 14

The Mounts of Jupiter

The mounts of Jupiter lie beneath the index or Jupiter fingers. They are roughly rectangular in shape and extend from the base of the first finger to the Head line, which forms their lower border. When normally developed they constitute low, rounded protrusions that are firm to the touch and pink in colour. They are overdeveloped or excessive when unduly prominent and underdeveloped or deficient when flat. A white or red colouration and a hard consistency are likewise negative features.

If both of your Jupiter mounts are normally developed you are warm, sociable and good-natured, and your ambitions are natural and healthy. You advance yourself by hard work, honest trading and enthusiasm. And because the mounts of Jupiter also symbolize religiosity, you are inherently God-fearing. When sited below Jupiter fingers that are too short, well-developed Jupiter mounts indicate that the ego is not as incompletely formed as the fingers alone would suggest. And similarly, when such mounts lie beneath Jupiter fingers that are too long they represent a moderation of the vanity and egotism suggested by the fingers.

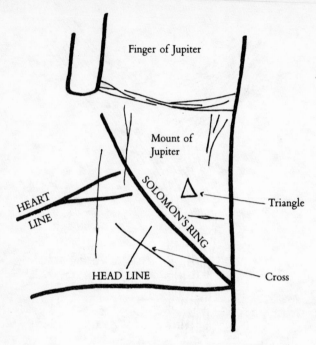

Figure 15

Overdeveloped mounts of Jupiter signify the person who is full of his own importance and who is vain, selfish and pompous. People like this tend to look down on others, which makes it difficult for them to have rewarding relationships. Hardly surprisingly, they are not the easiest people to work for as they enjoy wielding power. Very full Jupiter mounts also indicate greed and extravagance. These faults are at their maximum development when the Jupiter fingers are too long. Flat Jupiter mounts symbolize a weakly developed ego and thus low self-esteem, a lack of ambition and a nature that is easily influenced and manipulated. If flat Jupiter mounts accompany index fingers that are too short, the two together signify acute feelings of inferiority which are a serious impediment to the finding of happiness and success.

If the left Jupiter mount is normally developed but the right one deficient this shows that the natural or inborn self-confidence has been stifled by environmental factors. The converse is rarely found. A house cannot be built on quicksand.

The ego is most stable and confident when the apices of normally developed mounts of Jupiter are aligned with the centre of the index finger above them, as shown in Figure 16.

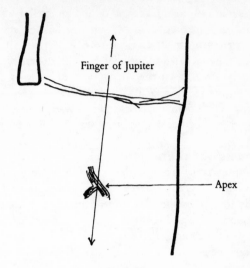

Finger of Jupiter

Apex

Figure 16

This placement of the apices also symbolizes honesty and integrity. However, when such centrally-sited apices are high-set they reveal greater conceit, the amount of which is measured by their closeness to the Jupiter fingers. Very full Jupiter mounts with high-set apices denote insufferable egotism. Lower-set apices show greater feelings for the family than the self and are thus indicative of pride in the family. Should the apices be displaced towards the mounts of Saturn they betoken dignity, seriousness and a rather high moral tone. Conversely, when the apices are displaced towards the side of the hands the personality is far more open and relaxed in its attitudes. If the apices lie close to the side of the hands the character is flighty and irresponsible.

Vertical lines appearing on the mounts of Jupiter are strengthening, representing as they do ego-stability and self-confidence. Transverse lines, however, detract from the positive indications of the mounts. They suggest a basic weakness of character.

You may possess a line which rises from the start of the Head line and which curves up across your Jupiter mounts to end between the index and middle fingers. This is known as the ring of Solomon or the line of renunciation. It is a very fortunate marking as it symbolizes, when fully developed, a rejection of the world and material values and, in turn, heightened spirituality. For this reason it is most commonly found on the hands of those who have taken religious vows. When it is half formed it indicates a lack of interest in money and possessions and a questioning, philosophical mind.

A cross is also sometimes found on the mounts of Jupiter and when present it symbolizes good fortune in marriage. Less frequently, the cross bears side arms and takes the form of a swastika, an ancient symbol of the Sun. The swastika shows that its bearer is lucky, particularly in educational matters and in the achievement of his goals. Those with this sign always manage to rise above adversity.

The ring of Solomon, the cross and the swastika are most fortunate in meaning when they occur on both mounts of Jupiter.

The Mounts of Saturn

The mounts of Saturn lie beneath the middle or Saturn fingers, and are, like the other finger mounts, rectangular in shape. Their lower border is effectively formed by the Heart line. One of the main palm lines, the Fate or Saturn line, usually runs up onto them. A semicircular line known as the ring of Saturn may also be present. The placement of the mount apices should be noted. These features and lines are illustrated in Figure 17.

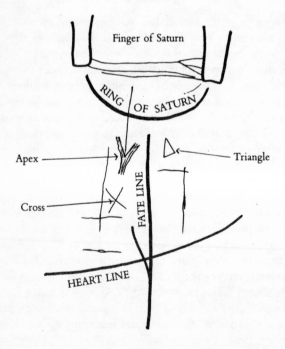

Figure 17

The two mounts of Saturn form low, gently rounded protrusions when they are normally developed and are firm to the touch and pink in colour. As such they symbolize emotional balance, mental order and a common-sense attitude to life. If your Saturn mounts are so developed you are prudent, patient, sober, dependable, studious and have a love of the land and of animals.

Overdeveloped mounts of Saturn are indicative of inner disquiet and thus a nature that is disordered and unhappy. Like Silas Marner before he was robbed of his gold and found Eppie, those with too prominent Saturn mounts are miserly and misanthropic, and their own interests are of paramount concern to them. They are also critical and suspicious. When prominent Saturn mounts accompany abnormally long Saturn fingers they signify paranoia.

Flat mounts of Saturn, especially if they are white in colour, reveal a low vitality and a lack of confidence and self-control. Those possessing deficient Saturn mounts tend to be contrary and easily influenced, and because these traits hinder them achieving their goals they become despondent and bitter as they age.

Vertical lines appearing on the Saturn mounts are positive in meaning, adding as they do to the strength of the mounts. The most important line of this type is the Fate or Saturn line itself, which runs up onto them from lower down on the palms. Because the Fate lines symbolize career progress their presence augments the Saturn mounts' indications of stablity and industry. However, because three or more vertical lines represent a variety of interests they do warn that career success may be adversely affected by a failure to specialize.

Transverse lines are, as we have seen, weakening or negative markings. Indeed, the ring of Saturn, when it is present, must be regarded as such a line, indicating as it does fecklessness and irresponsibility, and an absence of any clear purpose in life. A cross appearing on the Saturn mounts is also negative in meaning as it presages misfortune in business and sometimes a fatal accident. However, a cross should only be interpreted in the latter sense if the hands show other signs representative of sudden and perhaps premature death.

The placement of the Saturn mount apices must also be considered. If they are aligned with the centre of the Saturn fingers they symbolize a sensible, practical attitude to money and thus financial caution. Displaced towards the mounts of Jupiter, the apices signify self-confidence and an interest in acquiring riches, while their displacement towards the mounts of Apollo denotes financial irresponsibility, notably a weakness for spending money on or investing in the arts. High-set apices are a sign of ambition and drive; their owners are self-motivated. Low-set apices symbolize a desire to invest in land and property, to feel secure in terms of acres, bricks and mortar.

The Mounts of Apollo

The mounts of Apollo or the Sun are located beneath the third or Apollo
fingers. They are rectangular in shape and their lower border is formed
by the Heart line. An important palm line, the line of Apollo, often runs
up onto them. Marks like the star, cross and triangle are also sometimes
found. The mount and its lines and markings are shown in Figure 18.

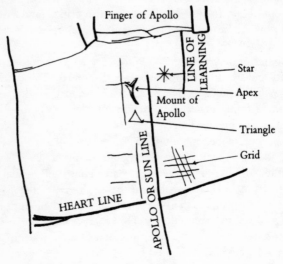

Figure 18

Your Apollo mounts should ideally be gently rounded, firm but not
hard and pink in colour. If they are you have a bright, outgoing
personality, a generous nature and good health. You are fun to be with
and as a consequence have many friends and an active social life. Your
social success is underscored by your intuitive understanding of others,
which makes you considerate and well mannered. You are interested in
the arts and you may be creative. Other positive hand features, such as
an outer bulge of your Moon mounts, will show how creative you are.

When the Apollo mounts are prominent they are to be considered
overdeveloped. Any mount excess betokens selfishness, which manifests
as vanity, foppishness and artistic egotism when the Apollo mounts are
large. Those with prominent Apollo mounts long for public recognition
and for this reason fall easy prey to flatterers. Their manner of dress tends
to be consciously arty, their impulses extravagant and their attitudes
snobbish.

Flat mounts of Apollo indicate a quieter, less showy personality and a weaker constitution. Because the Sun rules the heart, flat Apollo mounts are suggestive of possible heart problems, particularly if they are hard and white in colour or if they bear transverse lines and other negative markings. Deficient Apollo mounts also reveal a lack of interest in the arts and an impaired intuitive sense.

Vertical lines on the Apollo mounts are generally positive in meaning. The most important of these is the Apollo line itself, which presages good fortune and success in most areas of life if the Apollo mounts are normally developed. If there are two other vertical lines, one on either side of the Apollo line, they enhance an already fortunate marking. Yet more than three vertical lines symbolize too many interests and thus point to a want of success because of this.

A star is a favourable sign when it is found on the mounts of Apollo, particularly if it lies at the end of the Apollo line, where it signifies fame and wealth although not much happiness. Elsewhere, it indicates distinction and renown, which are gained at the expense of peace of mind. The triangle is therefore a better marking, for while it does not augur as much success it reveals greater contentment. A cross on the Apollo mounts is negative as it represents a failure to achieve one's ambitions. A grid symbolizes the desire to be famous but not the attainment of fame.

The apex of each Apollo mount should be aligned with the centre of the third fingers. When such centrally-placed apices are high-set they signify artistic creativity. But when low-set they indicate a preoccupation with health and hygiene, and hence a reduced satisfaction with life. Lying towards the mounts of Mercury, the apices betoken a sharp business sense, a love of travel and children, and a charming manner. If they are displaced towards the mounts of Saturn, the apices signify a more serious nature and, where art is concerned, a greater interest in staging and set design than in the artistic work they embellish.

The Mounts of Mercury

The Mounts of Mercury lie beneath the fourth or Mercury fingers, sandwiched as it were between those fingers and the mounts of Upper Mars, their lower border formed by the Heart line. A palm line known as the line of Mercury or line of Health often terminates on them. They may also bear marks like the star, triangle, cross and grid. These should be identified and properly evaluated, as should the placement of the mounts' apices.

Normally developed mounts of Mercury are, like the other mounts that lie beneath the fingers, low, gently rounded prominences that are

firm and pink in colour. Should yours be so formed you have a quick
wit, an optimistic spirit and a persuasive tongue. You also love travel,
change, novelty and adventure, and you have a flair for science. Thus it
is hardly surprising that those with well-developed Mercury mounts
make good salesmen, diplomats, lawyers, travel agents, teachers, actors,
businessmen and scientists.

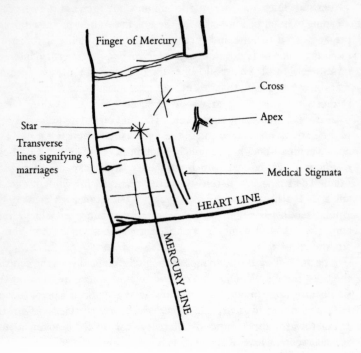

Figure 19

If the Mercury mounts are large they betray selfishness and a
tendency therefore to misuse the associated powers of persuasion and
charm for personal gain. Indeed, when prominent Mercury mounts lie
below crooked fourth fingers they reveal incipient or actual criminality.
Should they be paired with short fourth fingers they signify impulsiveness
and a ready temper. Large Mercury mounts also signify a weakness for
drugs and alcohol.

Flat Mercury mounts indicate that the characteristics linked with
Mercury are undeveloped or absent. Thus those with such mounts tend
to be rather dull, pessimistic and lacking in enthusiasm. Their verbal
powers are poor and they may, if other signs in the hand are also
negatively formed, suffer from a speech impediment. Flat mounts also

symbolize a lack of talent for business, science and literature.

The mounts of Mercury are strengthened by one, two or three vertical lines. Hence a flat mount with vertical lines reveals a more positive and enthusiastic nature than the mount itself does. Two or three vertical lines, lying wholly on the Mercury mounts, form what is known as the Medical Stigmata, which is a mark symbolizing medical skill or talent. It is often therefore seen in the hands of doctors, surgeons, nurses and veterinarians. The line of Mercury, which relates to the health, is discussed in a later chapter.

Transverse lines on the Mercury mounts are negative in meaning. They indicate anxiety, uncertainty and an inability to cope. Should they cross several vertical lines to form a grid they betoken an unstable temperament and dishonesty.

It is important, however, to distinguish between those transverse lines that lie wholly on the Mercury mounts and those that run onto them from the side of the hand or the percussion, as the latter are known as the lines of Marriage and are not, in themselves, negative.

If a star is found on the mounts of Mercury it represents success in either business or in some other Mercurian activity like law and science. A triangle, when present, has a similar meaning, although the promise portended is not so great. Yet it does signify more emotional fulfilment than the star. A cross is a negative sign and is the mark of a dishonest and unscupulous person.

Unlike the apices of the other mounts, those of the Mercury mounts should ideally be aligned with the inside edge of the fourth fingers, where they symbolize a healthy balance between intellect and intuition. Should the apices lie closer to the Apollo mounts they show more intuitive awareness and also art-related business interests. When displaced towards the side of the hands, the apices reveal a more rational hard-nosed business sense. High-set apices represent literary talent, low-set apices emotional courage.

9

THE PALM LINES

Now that we have reached the stage at which we must consider the lines of the palm, we have come to that part of hand reading that most people regard as the central core of the subject. But as we have seen, and this should never be forgotten, hand reading is much more than the interpretation of the palm lines, important though these are. For the palm lines cannot, when considered on their own, give a full insight into character, health and fate. Such a judgement can only be obtained by a study of the hands as a whole.

If you now look at your own palms you will see that they bear a number of lines, perhaps indeed very many lines, some of which are longer and thicker than the others. The most important of the latter type of lines are illustrated in Figure 20. Anatomists call these lines the flexure creases, which suggests that they are caused by the flexing or bending of the hands. This notion, however, is incorrect because they only partially align themselves with the flexure sites of the hands. And anyhow, simple bending could not account for the many differences in line length, thickness, clarity, breaks and other features that these lines show on the hands of different people. Nor could it explain their fading away or sudden appearance.

Although science has yet to recognize it, the evidence gathered by hand readers over the centuries unequivocably indicates that the palm lines are so intimately linked with the physical and psychological nature of ourselves that they are clear symbols of this nature. But they can reveal more than just character and health, as they can, like the other features of the hands, show what is going to happen. Hence they reveal our fate. There is nothing magical or mysterious about this. After all, what happens to each of us is largely a product of our genes, our character and our educational opportunities, which determine what path in life we follow, how far along that road we will walk and whether or not the journey will be interrupted by illness or prematurely ended by

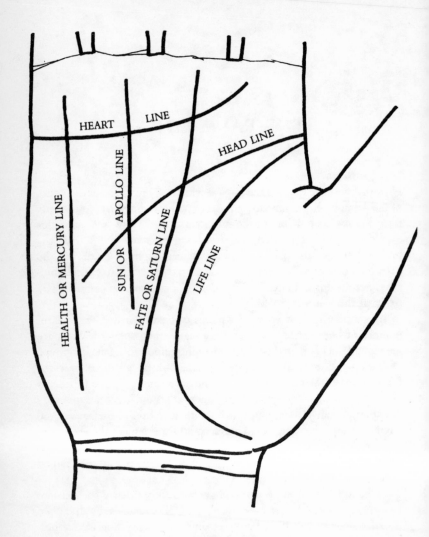

Figure 20

death. The happiness we get from life is largely of our own making, stemming as it does from the conditions that we help create around us. We may not be responsible, of course, for the accidents of life, which can either hurt us or lift us up, but otherwise we are very much the masters of our fate. We bring our troubles on our own heads, as Homer had Zeus observe in the Odyssey:

. . . O how falsely men
Accuse us Gods as authors of their ill!
When, by the bane their own bad lives instill,
They suffer all the miseries of their states,
Past our inflictions, and beyond their fates.

The Life Lines

The Life lines or the radial longitudinal lines of anatomy begin at the side of the hands above the thumb and, in their normal development, curve down the palm around the mounts of Lower Mars and the mounts of Venus. In fact they form the inner border of these mounts. The Life lines often end at the base of the mounts of Venus, when they are considered long. Short Life lines do not extend so far down the hand.

In common with the other palm lines, the Life lines, in their best form, should be clearly and quite deeply marked, unbroken and uncrossed by other lines, and free from islands and other defects. They should also curve boldly out into the hand to touch the palm's mid-point before sweeping back under the mounts of Venus. When so developed they betoken a strong, healthy constitution and a good vitality. In turn, such physical attributes suggest a long life.

For the second two-thirds of their length the Life lines mark the inner border of the mounts of Venus, which means that they are essentially a part of the Venus mounts, expressing what they say in a linear form. Thus the Life lines must be read with the mounts of Venus, for while the inward curve of the Life lines into the palms is a positive feature indicating physical vitality, this can only be developed to its optimum extent if the Venus mounts are well rounded, firm and of good colour.

If your Life lines do curve generously around the mounts of Venus, you may be interested to know that Indian tradition says that this signifies you were born when the Moon was waning. It also says that you will be healthy, happy and long lived.

It follows that when the mounts of Venus are narrow the Life lines are less curved, so that they will, after rounding the mounts of Lower Mars, descend almost vertically down the palm. When such lack of curvature is present it reflects a weaker constitution and a lower vitality. Those with Life lines of this type have a poorer resistance to disease and less energy. Furthermore, Life lines that bend around under the mounts of of Venus are one indicator of a stable and calm psychological state, which contrasts with that possessed by those whose Life lines incline towards the mounts of the Moon. Such a curve in the Life lines towards the intuitive side of the hands signifies a more excitable and instinctive psychological condition.

The Life lines usually begin at the side of the hands about midway between the Jupiter finger and the thumb. Sometimes, however, they commence from the Jupiter mounts themselves. When they do they reveal ambition and a strong desire to make an impression on the world. Such people may devote their lives to single-mindedly achieving their goals, which consequently makes them difficult to live with or work for. Their determined selfishness often brings them material rewards, but it is a sure sign of a basic unhappiness as it stems from an inner self-dissatisfaction.

Alternatively, a line may rise up from the Life lines to the mounts of Jupiter. If so, it is called the line of Jupiter and it betokens, not so much a sudden upsurge of ambition, but rather a movement up the ladder of success and the acquisition thereby of increased self-confidence. The age at which this step forward takes place is determined from the point on the Life lines that the line of Jupiter makes its appearance.

How then are events connected with the Life lines dated? This can be done quite easily, providing that the Life lines make a normal curve around the Venus mounts, because the furthest point that each line reaches out into the palm marks age fifty. If the distance between the start of the lines and this point is halved, this mid-point represents age twenty-five. By halving these portions of the lines we can then find age twelve and a half and thirty-seven and a half respectively. Further divisions can in turn give the exact year of age represented by the Life lines up until age fifty. But as the same time scale can be applied after this point, it enables us to date the whole of both Life lines. Thus a Jupiter line emerging from somewhere in the first inch of the Life lines would clearly represent an advance won during the school years, perhaps an examination success of some sort, especially as the mounts of Jupiter relate to education. However, when the Life lines descend the palm without curving then such time estimation is made more difficult and less precise.

This timing scheme makes a lot of sense as age fifty is a watershed in everyone's life, after which our strength and faculties diminish and we make a gradual descent into old age. Thus the Life lines can be visualized as pathways that have, like the celestial pathway of the Sun, an ascent or growth phase and a descent or contraction phase, along which our vital energy symbolically moves as the years pass.

Life lines that are weak in appearance or badly islanded, or broken, or crossed by several lines from the Venus mounts, naturally indicate a more delicate constitution and a lower vitality than those that are clearly marked and lacking in defects. Should the entire lines be badly formed, then the health remains poor throughout life. But more frequently the

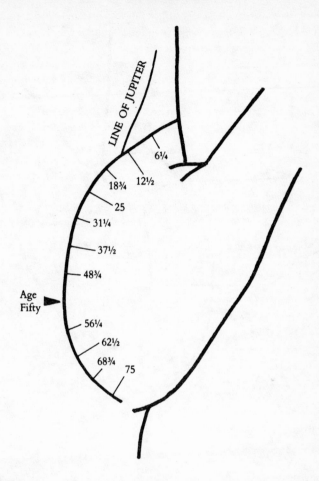

Figure 21

defects, when they are present, occur at specific points on the Life lines and refer to particular bouts of ill-health, whose occurrence can be dated in the manner outlined above.

The more common defects which may affect the Life line and the other palm lines are shown in Figure 22.

An island resembles a bubble and it is formed when a line splits apart for some distance and then rejoins. When found on the Life lines it always symbolizes a period of ill-health, which lasts for as long as the period of time covered by the island.

Sometimes a number of small islands link themselves together end to

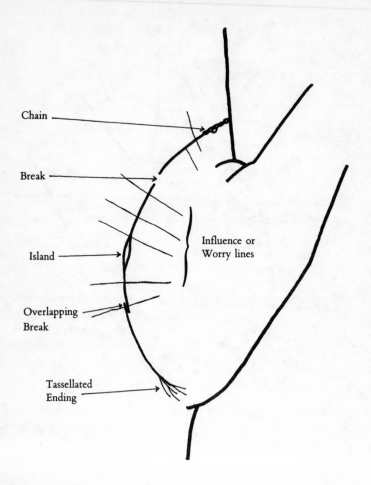

Chain

Break

Island

Overlapping
Break

Tassellated
Ending

Influence or
Worry lines

Figure 22

end to form what is known as a 'chain'. A chain also represents a period
of ill-health, but one that involves both mental and physical exhaustion.
When a chain is found at the start of the Life lines, like that shown in the
diagram above, it is often a sign of childhood pulmonary infections.

When a break occurs in the Life lines it indicates a health upset of
some seriousness that happens suddenly and unexpectedly, which may
be caused by a disease or an accident. But when the ends of the lines
overlap at the break, this reveals that the damage caused to the system is
far less severe than it might have been.

We cannot, however, accurately predict the nature of a disease condition from the Life lines alone, as breaks, islands and chains only indicate a period of ill-health and not its cause. Hence the nature of the disease can only be determined by examining the defects presented by the other hand parts. The two big killers of modern times are heart attacks and cancer. Heart disorders are symbolized by defects on the mounts of Apollo, the fingernails and the Heart lines; cancer, being a condition that can attack a variety of organs, such as the lungs, breasts and liver, is much harder to diagnose from the hands and for this reason is best left for the expert to uncover.

This brings us to the vexed question of whether or not the Life lines can tell us how long we are going to live. The answer to this is, paradoxically, yes and no. They can certainly tell us how long our physical condition will enable us to sustain life, which immediately tells us that short Life lines betoken a short life. Yet Life lines that are long do not necessarily mean a long life, because despite having a strong constitution our lives can be unnaturally shortened by accident, crime, suicide or by our own bad health habits. Thus although a long Life line is one sign that the life will be long, it must be supported by other positive features in the hands to make this certain.

Where length of life is concerned it is important to examine the Life lines of both hands. That of the left hand indicates our inherited or genetic strength and as such is the best guide to how much time we have been allotted. The right-hand Life line reveals the effects that our diet, upbringing, stress and bad habits like smoking have on our longevity. This is why the Life line of the right hand is rarely longer than that of the left and is frequently shorter.

But having ascertained how long your life could be, the next question that needs answering is 'How will I fare from a physical point of view in my later years?' After all, nobody relishes living to an advanced age if one has to spend it without one's faculties or sense.

The end of your life is symbolized, as might be expected, by the last portion of your Life lines. If these terminate as clear, well-formed lines unaffected by islands and other defects, while naturally becoming thinner as your batteries run down, then your old age will manifest as a slow, steady and dignified descent into dotage, with death coming peacefully and painlessly. A more difficult end is symbolized by islands or chains as these represent disease conditions, which must make the final years less graceful and dignified than you would like. And should the Life lines become frayed or tassellated at their ends, this shows that the last years will be adversely affected by physical degeneration or senile decay. Such a decline can, of course, be ameliorated to some extent by healthy living at an earlier age. Thus should your Life lines—

and the condition of the right-hand Life line is most important—show fraying at their ends you are advised to change your habits and your lifestyle so as to improve your physical state. This does not mean that you have to start jogging or lifting weights. The simple avoidance of stress, fatty foods, cigarettes or too much alcohol, combined with a brisk daily walk, will do wonders for your health.

Lines that rise upwards from the Life lines are known as effort lines and they are a positive feature of the hands, as are all ascending lines. We have already mentioned those that may rise to the mounts of Jupiter. Effort lines mark the beginning and the direction of successful moves forward in life, which can be dated from the point at which they start from the right-hand Life line. Should such a line ascend to the mount of Saturn it represents career success, symbolizing as it does the blossoming of your talents in a work-related sense. This line augments the Fate or Saturn line, or if the Fate line is absent, takes its place. Even greater success is augured by an effort line which rises to the mount of Apollo, for the laurels attained will be of an exceptional kind. And a line travelling to the mount of Mercury signifies success in business, science or politics, or in some other field ruled by Mercury.

Much less positive in meaning are those lines that cross the Life lines from the mount of Venus, as these symbolize worries and other adverse influences that can adversely affect your health and happiness. Health problems are indicated if the Influence lines break or otherwise impede the course of the Life lines.

Quite often another line, which usually originates on the mounts of Lower Mars, runs down across the Venus mounts inside the Life lines, appearing to be, in fact, almost like another Life line. This is called the line of Mars. It adds to the strength of the Life lines and thus indicates a stronger and more vigorous constitution than the Life lines themselves suggest. Such a fortified constitution remains intact for as long as the Mars lines accompany the Life lines, but weakens after it terminates.

Finally, Indian tradition says that when a single island appears at the start of the Life line of the right hand it symbolizes illegitimacy, while such an island when present at the beginning of the left-hand Life line symbolizes adoption. It also says that when a light-coloured mole lies on the Life line—its presence on that of the right hand is best—it signifies a happy life.

The Head Lines
The Head lines, which are known to anatomists as the proximal or lower transverse lines, begin at the side of the hands below the index fingers and travel across the palms through the Plain of Mars. Their length and

degree of slope can vary considerably, which is not surprising in view of
the fact that they symbolize the type of mentality that we have. Badly
formed Head lines or those that show islands, breaks and other defects
point to mental deficiences of one sort or another, or at worst to actual
head or brain injuries.

As with the other palm lines, the Head lines should be clearly and
quite deeply marked, neither too thin nor too broad, and free of defects.
They should also run across the palms in a gentle curve to end at the
junction between the mounts of Upper Mars and the mounts of Luna.
Head lines like this represent an alert, quickly comprehending mind,
one possessed of both practical sense and intuitive understanding, a good
memory and a positive outlook.

However, because no hand feature should be judged in isolation, the
Head lines must be evaluated with reference to those parts of the hand
that also relate to mental functioning such as the fingers and, indeed,
the basic hand shape itself.

If you examine the start of each of your own Head lines you will see
that they may commence from the Life line or are separate from it, or
they rise from below the Life line on the mount of Lower Mars.

The point of origin of the Head lines symbolizes your degree of self-
confidence. Hence their commencement must be read with regard to
the length of the index fingers, which also relates to feelings of self-
worth.

When the Head lines touch, but are not tied to, the Life lines at their
beginning, or start from just above them, they reveal a healthy degree of
self-confidence and, as a consequence, an optimistic spirit. Such a person
is capable of making his own decisions and is not afraid of speaking his
mind.

But should the Head lines be tied to the Life lines for any length, this
cleaving or reluctance to break away from the Life lines symbolizes less
self-confidence, the lack of which is proportional to the length of the tie.
If the index fingers are also too short, the two features together indicate
an inferiority complex and pronounced feelings of inadequacy, which
must necessarily throw a shadow over the life.

Head lines which arise from the mounts of Lower Mars also reveal a
lack of confidence, but one that is associated with a strong sense of
grievance. They are thus the mark of the person with a chip on his
shoulder. Such an individual may, by way of compensation, become
involved with extreme political groups or with criminal activities that
give him or her a sense of power and self-worth.

When the Head lines are quite separate from the Life lines at their
start, this signifies over-confidence and brashness and as a consequence

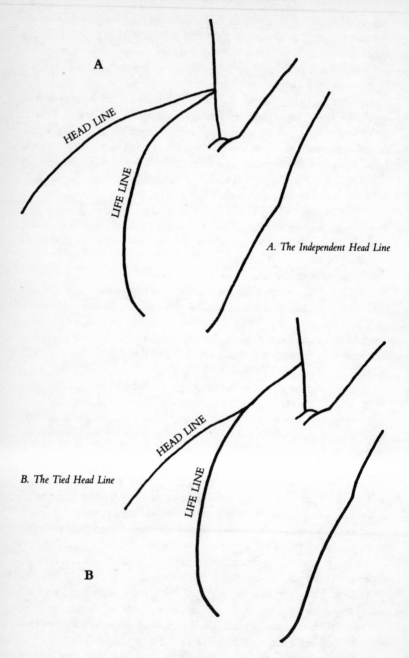

A. The Independent Head Line

B. The Tied Head Line

Figure 23

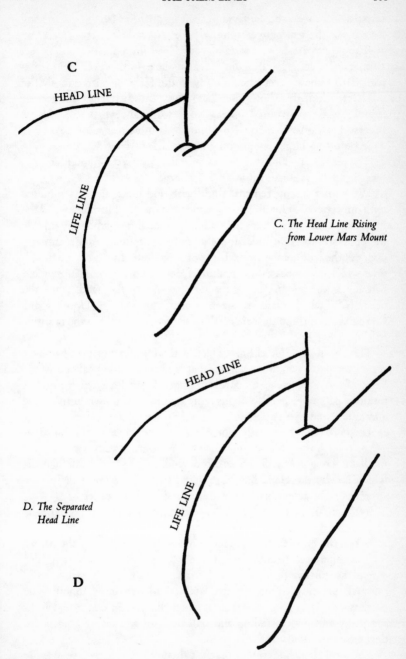

C

HEAD LINE

LIFE LINE

C. The Head Line Rising
from Lower Mars Mount

HEAD LINE

LIFE LINE

D. The Separated
Head Line

D

Figure 24

impulsive and erratic behaviour. These qualities are at their most extreme if the gap between the two lines is wide.

The point of origin of each of your Head lines must be compared. Both may, of course, start from the same place. If, however, your right-hand Head line cleaves more closely to the Life line than does that of your left hand, this shows the uncertainty and diffidence the former represents were acquired during your formative years. Should the reverse be the case, then your childhood influences allowed you to overcome to a large extent your inborn lack of confidence.

The length of your Head lines symbolizes how your mind functions, whether it be rational, intuitive or creative.

We earlier discovered that the thumb and index finger are linked with our rational or intellectual qualities and that the third finger and the little finger with our irrational or intuitive qualities, while the middle finger relates to both. Indeed, the palm beneath them can be similarly divided, the half below the mid-line of the middle finger on the thumb side, which encompasses the mounts of Venus, Lower Mars, Jupiter and half the Saturn mount, being the rational half of the hand, while the other half, which includes the mounts of the Moon, Upper Mars, Mercury, Apollo and the other half of the Saturn mount, is the intuitive half.

This means that Head lines which extend no further than half-way across the palm symbolize a mind that is rational or logical and which lacks intuitive or creative sparkle. Longer Head lines reach into the intuitive half of the hands and therefore symbolize a more intuitive mind and hence one that is potentially more creative.

Furthermore, abnormally short Head lines which do not extend as far across the palms as the second fingers are a sign of a low or restricted intellect. Long Head lines therefore symbolize creative intelligence, which is why the Head line of Albert Einstein, shown in Figure 25, stretches right across his palm from one side to the other.

Yet mental functioning is not only represented by the length of the Head lines, but by their slope as well.

When the Head lines travel more or less straight out into the palms, they betoken practicality unenlivened by imagination. If they also extend no further than half-way across the palms, they symbolize a rational, practical, unimaginative and calculative mind. Should the mounts of Venus also be deficient, then the person concerned lacks sympathy and understanding and will be hard and rather cold in his dealings with others.

The ideal Head lines run across the palm in a gentle slope to end at the junction between the mounts of Upper Mars and the mounts of Luna.

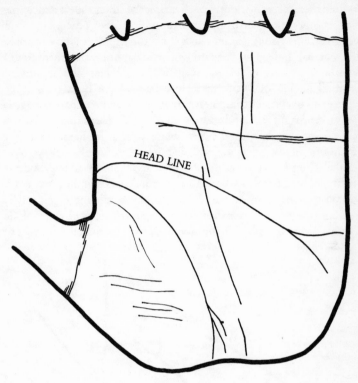

Figure 25

Lines of this type symbolize a mind that is both practical and imaginative, each quality being at the service of the other. However, should such curved Head lines extend no further than half-way across the palms, their slope indicates that while the person concerned lacks intuition his imagination is sufficient to temper the logical cast of his mind. Head lines that curve more sharply down into the hands symbolize a rich imagination but a deficient practical sense.

When the Head lines are sufficiently long and curved to reach the mounts of the Moon they reveal an intuitive mind that is over-endowed with imagination, perhaps to its detriment. Yet we must again distinguish between those Head lines that end at the top half of the Luna mounts, such as we see in the drawing of Albert Einstein's hand, and those that end at the bottom half of the Luna mounts. The former symbolize an imagination that is containable and thus a mind that is potentially very creative, while the latter represent an imagination that is out of control. Hence those with long and deeply sloping Head lines may find themselves in the grip of all manner of strange ideas and fancies that not only make it difficult for them to find inner peace, but which can, given the wrong circumstances, tip them into insanity or make them suicidal. Indeed, in standard works on palmistry sharply drooping Head lines are said to symbolize suicidal tendencies, although by no means all suicide victims possess Head lines of this type.

It is, of course, most important to examine and compare the Head lines of your right and left hands. Your left-hand Head line symbolizes your inherited mental tendencies, while your right-hand Head line shows how these tendencies have manifested.

It is also important to evaluate the ending of your Head lines and any defects like islands, chains, breaks, crosses and stars that they may have.

Head lines that terminate in a fork reveal a versatile nature, especially if the lines themselves are basically straight and the lower branch of the fork runs down towards or to the mounts of the Moon. In the drawing of

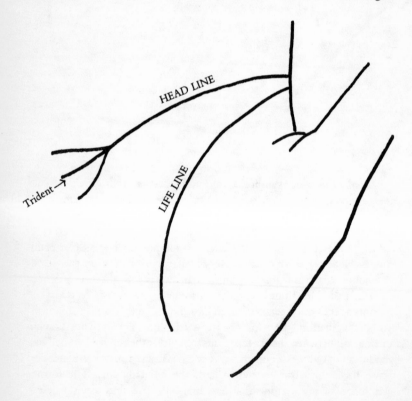

Figure 26

Albert Einstein's right hand, which was taken from a print, we can see that his long, sloping Head line ends on the mount of Luna, where it forks, the upper branch rising to cross the top half of the Moon mount to reach the side of the hand. The rising branch symbolizes his practical grasp of science and scientific method, which is complemented by his intuitive understanding of his subject, the two producing his genius.

Should the Head lines terminate in a trident, as shown in Figure 26, this is a most fortunate marking as it not only symbolizes a well-balanced mind, one endowed with practical ability, intuition and imagination, but it also portends better than average fortune in mental endeavours, which naturally suggests good luck in examinations, writing, business activities and so forth.

Islands appearing on the Head lines are never a good sign. They relate to periods of mental impairment, wherein the mind's grip on reality is diminished and which may be caused by high levels of stress. A chain of small islands symbolizes lack of concentration, memory failure, vacillation and worry. An island lying at the end of the Head lines portends mental impairment in later life. When it is partnered by frayed Life lines, the two together symbolize senile dementia.

Head lines that terminate in a cross symbolize a fatal head injury. A cross located at any other point on the Head lines also represents a head injury, although one that is not fatal, unless the Life lines are correspondingly short. Breaks in the Head lines also refer to head injuries, which may be, if supported by other negative indications, fatal.

When the Head lines end in a star this signifies insanity. If the Head lines are long and the star ending them lies on the mount of Luna, this betokens severe depression and sometimes schizophrenia. Should the Head lines be shorter and the star placed on the Plain of Mars, it is suggestive of manic-depressive psychosis, particularly if the Head lines curve downwards.

A star that terminates the left-hand Head line naturally symbolizes an inherited mental abnormality, which will only manifest itself if it is accompanied by a similar star in the right hand.

The Heart Lines
The Heart lines, which are technically called the upper or distal transverse lines, run across the palms above the Head lines from the percussion or outer edge of the hands to a point on or near the mounts of Jupiter. They are important because their course and nature reveals much about your emotional state and the health of your heart. They also symbolize your sexual type.

As with the other palm lines, and the point is well worth iterating, the

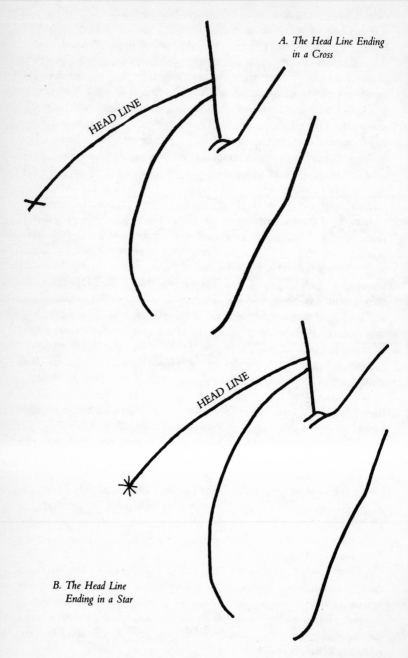

A. The Head Line Ending
in a Cross

HEAD LINE

HEAD LINE

B. The Head Line
Ending in a Star

Figure 27

Heart line of both hands should be clearly and quite deeply marked without being too thin or too broad, possess a pink colour and be free of any defects like islands, breaks, cross lines and so on. When so etched on the palms the Heart lines betoken a healthy heart and an efficient vascular system.

In India the Heart lines are known as the *Jivan rekhas* or Life lines and from them Indian palmists estimate the length of the life. There is much to commend this idea because life does end when the heart stops beating, and if the Heart lines can tell when that is going to happen they can certainly be used to predict our longevity. For best results, therefore, it is recommended that you determine the length of your own life from the length and quality of your Life lines, Head lines and Heart lines. If all are long and well formed they naturally indicate a generous life-span.

Indian palmists say that if the Heart lines extend from the percussion to the opposite side of the palms they promise a life lasting 100 years. Because the width of each mount effectively divides this distance into four, each quarter representing twenty-five years, this gives you an easy measure of how long your life will be as judged from the Heart lines. Thus Heart lines that travel from the side of the hands to the far edge of the mounts of Saturn mark out a life-span of seventy-five years; if to the mid-point of the Saturn mounts, a life-span of sixty-three years; and if only to the far edge of the Apollo mounts a life-span of fifty years, and so on. As with the Life lines, it is the right-hand Heart line that is most important when estimating longevity. However, do remember that the Heart-line length is only an accurate indicator of longevity if the lines themselves are clearly marked and free from breaks and other defects.

Two other distances are also important where the Heart lines are concerned. The first, marked A in Figure 28, is that between the Heart lines and the base of the fingers, and the second, marked B, is that between the Heart lines and the Head lines.

When the Heart lines are deeply placed on the hands, so that the distance between them and the fingers is wide, they symbolize a warm, generous and sympathetic disposition and thus a concern for others. The higher the lines are set and the narrower the gap between them and the fingers, so the nature becomes more selfish, colder and less charitable.

In a similar way, a wide space between the Heart lines and the Head lines betokens a broad mind, unconventional attitudes and altruism. A narrow gap between the two lines suggests the opposite: narrow views, conventionality and an introverted, selfish tendency. It also signifies a predisposition to asthma, which is hardly surprising in view of the disease's known emotional base.

Should the distance between the Heart lines and the base of the

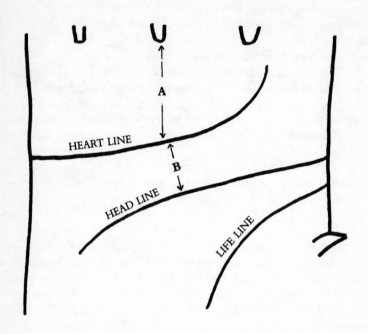

Figure 28

fingers be broad and that between them and the Head lines be narrow, this indicates that the sympathy and generosity exuded by the subject is calculated and is generated for selfish ends. People of this type use niceness to get what they want.

These aspects of the personality are also alluded to by the termination points of the Heart lines. At one extreme they may cross half the palms and then curve up strongly to end on the mounts of Saturn (line ABC in Figure 29) or between the mounts of Saturn and Jupiter (line ABD). At the other they may cross the palms in a straight line and then droop downwards, perhaps to touch or even pass beyond the Head lines (line ABG). Or they may, if they are of sufficient length, end at any point on the mounts of Jupiter (lines ABF).

Heart lines that curve upwards reveal a masculine or physical sexual tendency and those that are straight or bend downwards a feminine or mental sexual tendency. People of the first type are excited by

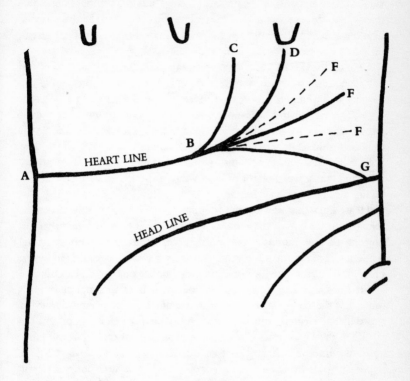

Figure 29

straightforward sexual stimuli—thoughts of the sex act, erotic pictures, the presence of the opposite sex, etc.—and those of the second by more complex, less straightforward stimuli, such as music, poetry, clothing, mental images, arty pictures and the like. Baldly stated, the first are easily aroused and quickly gratified, while the second need more time and have romantic requirements that must be satisfied before sexual intercourse is desired or allowed.

Hence when the Heart lines curve strongly upwards to end on the mounts of Saturn (line ABC), they betoken a sexual nature that is very physical and in turn the person who puts his sex needs before those of the partner. Such a person is passionate and easily aroused, yet is selfish and demanding in the act of love. His (or her) strong urges may result in sexual deviance if the Saturn mounts themselves are either over-developed or underdeveloped, the former signifying the potential rapist and the latter the self-abuser and pervert.

Heart lines that end between the mounts of Saturn and Jupiter also symbolize a masculine or physical sexual nature, although one less selfish than that represented by Heart lines that rise to the Saturn mounts. This termination also indicates, like Heart lines that are low-set, a warm, vital and generous disposition.

Should the Heart lines fork at their ends, one branch rising up between the mounts of Saturn and Jupiter, the other ending on the mounts of Jupiter, this reveals a more complex sexual and emotional type. The personality has both masculine and feminine tendencies, which may, in some individuals, manifest as bisexuality, although it usually produces a more rounded and balanced sexual nature. The branch to the Jupiter mounts signifies a more idealistic attitude, implying that sex is thought of in terms of a specific individual and as a loving act, not one of conquest.

Heart lines that end on the mounts of Jupiter are gently curved if they rise to the top of the mounts, but straight if they terminate on the bottom of the mounts. The former represent a masculine sexual tendency of moderate dimensions, the latter a feminine sexual tendency. However, because the Jupiter mounts symbolize our ego and ambitions, Heart lines that rise to the upper, mental half of the Jupiter mounts show that the choice of partner is determined by status considerations and will be selected from a narrow social or financial group.

When the Heart lines end on the bottom half of the Jupiter mounts their straightness indicates that mood, feelings and romance play an important part in any intimate encounter. But as such long, straight Heart lines also reveal a more cautious and more demanding nature, one in which mental considerations play as large a part as love and physical desire, such types rarely get swept off their feet. However, because straight Heart lines also betoken a jealous temperament their owners are easily hurt by real or imagined slights.

If the Heart lines droop downwards to touch the Head lines or throw down a branch to them, they show that the emotions are strongly influenced by the intellect with regard to what is right and proper, which can be a positive feature of the personality if this moderates sexual needs but not if it prevents a proper expression of the sexuality.

Lastly, should the Heart lines curve downwards and cross both the Head lines and Life lines to end on the mounts of Lower Mars, or send a branch to these mounts, this symbolizes a deep emotional hurt that has thrown a shadow over the life. This may have resulted from the loss of one or both parents at an early age, from psychological or sexual abuse experienced during childhood, or more simply from a traumatic love affair. But whatever the cause, the emotions have been badly damaged and the personality negatively affected, which means that the person concerned finds it difficult to establish successful and loving relationships with others, and so to achieve happiness and personal fulfilment.

Shorter Heart lines that fail to reach the mounts of Jupiter are indicative of both a shorter life and a more introverted and calculating emotional make-up, especially if they end on or below the mounts of Saturn. It has also been said that short Heart lines signify a smaller heart, although this has not been fully verified. If the Heart lines are thin it is a sign of emotional coldness.

It is not favourable from a fortune aspect for the Heart lines to terminate as a single line, as this portends a lack of financial success and, quite often, a failure to have children. More favourable are Heart lines that end in a fork because this signifies both a well-balanced emotional nature, and thus better fortune in love and marriage, and good prospects generally.

However, the most fortunate Heart lines terminate in a trident on the mounts of Jupiter. These promise a happy life, a loving marriage and material success. You are blessed indeed if your Heart lines show such an ending!

When the Heart lines are broken or bear islands and other defects these symbolize potential or actual heart trouble. But again, such defects must not be judged in isolation but with regard to the other hand parts that relate to the heart. Defects of the left-hand Heart line symbolize inborn heart weaknesses. If similar defects are absent from the right-hand Heart line this indicates that the quality of the lifesyle has prevented these weaknesses from manifesting as a physical impairment or disease.

A clear break in the right-hand Heart line is suggestive of a sudden upset in heart function, which usually means a heart attack. The age at which this will occur can be determined from the position of the break in the line. Should the Life line end at the same age, the heart attack will prove fatal. Overlapping breaks in the right-hand Heart line represent milder, non-fatal heart attacks.

If the left-hand Heart line bears a chain of islands this reveals an inborn predisposition to such ailments as angina, cardiac thrombosis and coronary thrombosis. These, however, will only develop and negatively affect the health if a chain is also present in the right-hand Heart line. If a chain is found only in the right-hand Heart line it symbolizes a heart weakness that has been caused by bad living habits, such as smoking heavily and failing to exercise. Heart lines that are red in colour betoken an excitable disposition, which may in itself adversely affect the functioning of the heart.

Single islands in the Heart lines have to be judged by their position as they often refer to diseases or to physical disorders that are not connected with the heart. A single island placed beneath the mounts of Mercury, for example, is a sign of mouth and tongue ailments. A single island lying below the mounts of Apollo symbolizes eye problems, while a single island sited below the Saturn mounts indicates stomach and intestinal disorders. However, a single island found below the Jupiter mounts is indicative of potential or actual arterial malfunctioning.

The Fate Lines

The Fate or Saturn line runs up the centre of the palms towards or to the mounts of Saturn. Its length and position account for its anatomical name—the long longitudinal line—although these vary greatly from person to person. Indeed, it is sometimes completely absent in both hands. This is why it became associated with fate or destiny, which is different for everyone.

Ideally, however, the Fate lines should be long and clearly marked, unbroken, uncrossed by lines other than the Head and Heart lines, and free from defects like islands. They should be neither too broad nor too deeply cut into the palms, and their colour should be a healthy pink. In their best development they are branched like a tree, the branches rising to the other finger mounts. Because the Fate lines symbolize the path down which we travel in life, their starting point in the hands represents the age at which we begin life on our own account. Hence the lower they rise on the hands, the earlier does our independence commence. And similarly, the higher on the hands they end the longer the urge to achieve continues and the longer we remain busy. Thus a full working life is symbolized by Fate lines that start low down on the palms and which terminate high up on the mounts of Saturn.

The Fate line of your left hand reveals your career or work potential, that of your right hand how this potential is developed. The differences that exist between these two lines represent the difference between what might have been and what was, is and will be.

Figure 30 illustrates the main points of origin of the Fate line.

If your right-hand Fate line begins low down on your palm (line A-F in the diagram) it shows that you made an early and independent start to your career. However, should the line start from the wrist lines or racettes this symbolizes childhood difficulties that may either rob the line of its promise or prevent you from finding happiness.

Because birth is represented by the topmost racette and the age thirty-five by the point at which the Fate lines cross the Head line, this makes timing by the Fate line easy. Thus if the right-hand Fate line

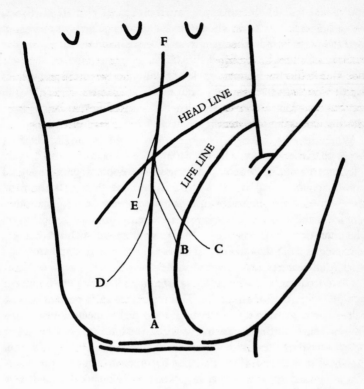

Figure 30

begins midway between these two places it shows that independence was gained at about seventeen-and-a-half years of age. A lower start would necessarily indicate a greater precocity, either in the sense of the person concerned setting his or her career goals at a young age or by actually starting work prior to leaving school.

An island is sometimes found at the start of the Fate lines. When present it is an unfortunate sign as it indicates the loss of both parents during infancy or early childhood.

If your right-hand Fate line starts low down on your hand and then travels to the Saturn mount, and is clearly marked, unbroken and branched, it promises a successful career, particularly if the other hand features are good.

Quite often, however, the right-hand Fate line commences from the Life line (line B–F), in which case it takes the form of an effort line rising from the Life line. Such an origin represents a less certain and more restricted career start and thus a lack of independence in the early part of life. A tied Fate line of this type usually indicates close family links, which suggests that, even when independence is gained, a connection with the parents and other family members is maintained.

Occasionally the right-hand Fate line begins on the mount of Venus (line C–F). This is not a favourable beginning for the line as it indicates that the course of the life will be negatively swayed by a desire for the opposite sex. Men suffering from the Casanova syndrome often have Fate lines showing this commencement.

When the Fate line begins on the mount of the Moon (line D–F) it shows that the destiny will be variable and uncertain and largely determined by other people. Yet because the Moon mounts are linked with imagination and art, a right-hand Fate line that starts from the Moon mount often indicates an artistic or literary career. The 'other people' in this respect are therefore the agents, producers and buyers who guide or promote the artist's life. How successful such a career will be is judged from the quality and course of the Fate line and from the other hand features that relate to success.

More frequently, however, a less prominent line runs up to join the Fate line from the Moon mount. This represents an important outside influence coming into the life at the age at which it meets the Fate line. This influence is often a husband or wife, which is why the line can be read as a marriage line, although confirmation of this should be sought elsewhere in the hand. If the Fate line becomes stronger in appearance after it is joined by the influence line, then the person involved will have a positive effect on the career. But if the fate line weakens or degenerates after that point then he or she will have a negative influence on the life and career generally.

Less commonly found is the right-hand Fate line that starts from the Plain or Triangle of Mars (line E–F). Because Mars is the planet of strife and difficulty, such a Fate line beginning reveals that the early years were tough for the person concerned and that his or her efforts to get on went unrewarded until the age at which the Fate line makes its appearance. His or her subsequent progress must be judged from the clarity, course and freedom from defects of the Fate line and by the presence of other favourable features, such as good Sun lines. If these are supportive and if the Fate line is well marked, the career will develop successfully after a difficult start.

However, if the right-hand Fate line travels directly to the mount of Saturn from whatever starting point in the hand and shows no branches to the other mounts, it does not augur great success but rather a life of steady plodding. Such a life may bring satisfaction but will have no highlights, and to those who have Fire hands, which are the mark of an outgoing and ambitious character, a Fate line of this type naturally suggests frustration and disappointment. Yet should the line be accompanied by other favourable features, like a good Sun line, then rewards will come at the time that these appear.

Sometimes an unbranched right-hand Fate line does not end on the Saturn mount, but on one of the other mounts. Such a deviation in course gives the line greater promise.

If the Fate line terminates on the mount of Jupiter it signifies a rise to a position of power and influence, which means that its owner will become someone of importance. When the Fate line ends on the mount of Apollo it indicates that the person concerned will become well known through his work, that he or she may become wealthy and that the career will be artistic or creative in nature. And should the Fate line end on the mount of Mercury it shows that success will come in business or science. This Fate line ending is also a sign of shrewdness and financial talent.

The principal negative features of the Fate lines are shown in Figure 31. They are the bar, island, break and star.

The Fate lines are ordinarily crossed by two palm lines, the Head line and the Heart line, neither of which has any special meaning unless the Fate line is terminated by them or if a defect like an island appears in the Fate line at the point where the lines cross it. But when short bar lines lie across the Fate lines these represent obstacles standing in the way of career progress that have to be surmounted at the time of life at which they appear. These obstacles are serious if they break the Fate lines or if they coincide with an island.

A break in the Fate line of the right hand symbolizes a sudden interruption of the career, which lasts for as long as the break does. Should the break be crossed by a down-drooping line from the Heart line, this signifies that emotional problems stemming from a romantic involvement are the cause of the upset. A break associated with a similar line coming from the Head line reveals that mental difficulties or bad decisions are responsible for the setback. A break or breaks linked with bar lines relate to career upsets caused by outside factors that are not under the person's control.

The above refers to clean breaks in the Fate line. Overlapping breaks are more positive in meaning as they refer to changes in the course of the career which happen smoothly.

An island is always a negative sign wherever it is found on the Fate line and we have already noted that an island situated at the start of the line symbolizes the early death of the parents. Placed higher up the line, the island represents financial difficulties and the worry occasioned by these. The difficulties begin at the age indicated by the lower end of the

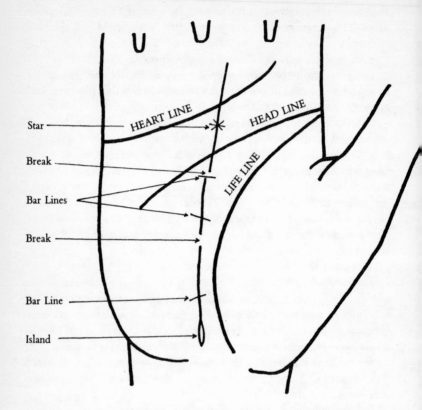

Figure 31

island and endure for as long as the island lasts. Extended career and financial problems are symbolized by a chain, which is therefore a very negative Fate line feature. If an island appears at the end of the Fate line, it shows that the final years of the career will be spoiled by setbacks and gloom.

The star is never a favourable sign when it lies on the Fate line, as it represents a dramatic and hard-to-right upset. The time that this happens is indicated by the placement of the star on the line. The upset symbolized by the star brings heavy financial losses or bankruptcy, but if the Fate line is clearly marked after the star and either branched or supported by a good Sun line, then the career will be successfully resumed after a period of struggle and readjustment.

Ideally, the right-hand Fate line should run directly to the Saturn mount and send branches to one or more of the other finger mounts. But if it follows a sinuous course and be unbranched, it shows that the career path will be uncertain and lacking in direction. Thus, a crooked Fate line portends a troubled career.

If the Fate line travels to the Saturn mount and also sends a branch to the mount of Jupiter, this indicates that its owner will rise high in life through hard work and come to occupy a position of power and influence. And because the Jupiter mount symbolizes the needs of the ego, such a branch reveals that the ambitions are satisfied.

Should a branch from the Fate line rise to the mount of Apollo it indicates that, especially if the other hand features are positive, the subject will achieve fame and wealth. Hardly surprisingly, many successful artists and entertainers have such a branch line in their hands.

Lastly, if the Fate line sends a branch to the mount of Mercury, then success will be obtained in business, science or in the media. The area of expertise can be determined from the basic hand shape and from other hand features.

The most successful person from a career point of view has a Fate line which shows no defects and which travels in a straight well-marked course to the Saturn mount, sending a branch to each of the other finger mounts. The man or woman so blessed will rise to an eminent position and become wealthy, respected and highly praised, particularly if his or her Fate line is accompanied by other fortunate markings. It is, however, rare to come across such a fully-branched Fate line and even more unusual to find a combination of fortunate signs. This is because such positive features are only possessed by the most successful people.

The Fate line may not reach the Saturn mount, in which case it indicates that the career will be shorter than normal. This may be caused by marriage, ill-health or childbirth, all of which are symbolized by other hand markings. But if the Fate line terminates at the Head line it shows that a major error of judgement brings the career to an end. Similarly, if the Fate line ends at the Heart line it reveals that the career is halted by a bitter disappointment in love.

Two Fate lines are sometimes found running side by side up the centre of the hand. If these are equally well marked and if they each run to a different finger mount, they symbolize two careers that are followed at the same time. But if one of the lines is weaker in form it represents a hobby or interest which, while pursued with vigour, is necessarily of secondary importance. However, should this line thicken or branch higher up the hand, or if it continues after the main Fate line has ended, it shows that the hobby will turn into a major source of satisfaction later in life. A second Fate line is therefore frequently found in the hands of those who have an artistic hobby to which they devote all their time after they retire.

The Sun Lines

The Sun or Apollo line is a vertical line which runs up the palms to the mount of Apollo. It is also called the line of success. In India it is known as the *Dharm rekha* or line of righteousness. If the other hand features and lines be good, the presence of a straight, clearly marked and unbroken Sun line on the right hand promises success, wealth, fame and happiness. It is therefore a sign of superior personal achievement.

The Sun lines also naturally express those qualities associated with the Sun: youthfulness, health, confidence and vitality. Hence good Sun lines symbolize a positive and zestful nature. When they are absent, the character is necessarily more pessimistic and less self-assured.

In its best development the right-hand Sun line starts low down on the hand near the wrist and proceeds in a straight course to the mount of Apollo. If the other hand features are supportive, such a line represents a very clever mind and an outstanding character, and the acquisition of

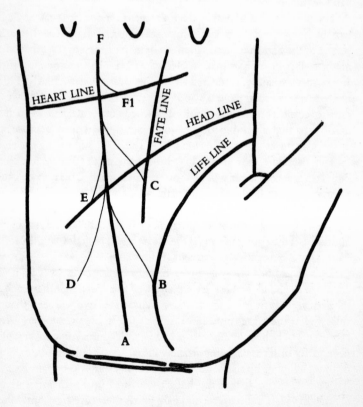

Figure 32

wealth and fame at an early age. Hence it is rare to find a Sun line so fully developed, as it only appears on the hands of exceptional men and women. Yet a long Sun line always indicates a brilliant life, even though it may not start so far down in the hand.

Like the Fate lines, the Sun lines can begin from a variety of positions on the palms. The main points of commencement are shown in Figure 32.

A Sun line that runs up the palm from its base (line A-F) is its ideal form. It is, as was mentioned above, a rare and special mark.

Also seldom found is the Sun line that starts from the Life line (line B-F), in which case it takes the form of an effort line rising from the Life line. This symbolizes a much more fortunate period of existence which begins at the age indicated by its emergence from the Life line. In this respect it is similar to a Fate line which rises from the Life line, although the Sun line has greater promise. However, its promise will only be realized if it is clearly marked, unbroken and uncrossed by other lines, and if the hands show other good features.

The line of the Sun may also start from the Fate line (line C-F), when it can also be regarded as a branch of the Fate line rising to the Apollo mount. As such, it reveals that from the age as determined by its starting point on the Fate line, the career blossoms and becomes generally more successful. It therefore augurs wealth, fulfilment and a measure of fame. It also symbolizes greater happiness from that point in time on.

When the Sun line travels from the mount of the Moon to the Apollo mount (line D-F) it serves as a connecting channel between the two mounts, thereby uniting the qualities of each. And as the Luna mount symbolizes imagination and creativity when well developed, a Sun line originating there indicates that success may come from literary or artistic pursuits and that the career will be helped and guided by others. Also, because the Sun and Moon mounts respectively symbolize the twin poles of existence, masculine and feminine, good and evil, light and darkness, etc., those with these mounts linked by a Sun line have strong and rather remarkable characters, whose powers can either be used to benefit mankind or to harm it, depending upon the influences to which they are subject.

If the right-hand Sun line takes its start from the Head line (line E-F), this shows that success will come from an idea or breakthrough originated by its owner. The timing of such an advance must be judged either from an effort line ascending from the Life line or from a branch of the Fate line. These lines should ideally travel to either the Apollo mount or the mount of Mercury.

Quite often the Sun line is short in length as it rises from the Heart line (line F^1–F). If it then runs to the top of the Apollo mount and is straight and unbroken, it signifies happiness and material success later in life. And because the Heart line symbolizes love and the emotions, a Sun line starting from it often represents a positively influential love affair or marriage. Confirmation of this must be looked for in the Marriage lines and in any line travelling from the mount of Luna to the Fate line.

Eventual success is also signified by an Apollo line that begins from the Plain of Mars, although as with the Fate line that starts there such success only comes after a hard struggle and much disappointment.

In rare instances the Sun line itself branches to form a trident, one branch extending to the mount of Saturn, the central branch ending on the Apollo mount and the third branch terminating on the mount of Mercury. This is an extremely fortunate marking and adds considerably to the Sun line's promise, indicating as it does great fame, wealth and happiness. It is therefore found only on the hands of those who are destined to become exceptional people.

Sometimes the Sun line terminates in a trident on the Apollo mount itself. This is also a special marking, indicating as it does the acquisition of wealth and fame through one's own efforts. Likewise, two sister lines are occasionally found accompanying the Sun line, one running along each side of it, and when present they greatly enhance the meaning of the Sun line and portend remarkable success. When such sister lines occur with a Sun line ending in a trident, the two together symbolize the greatest celebrity, wealth and success.

A branched Sun line is always more favourable than a single line, no matter how straight and clearly marked the latter may be. A branched Sun line is a sure sign of riches and fame, providing, of course, that the hands are fortunate in other respects.

Similarly, when the Sun line terminates in a star this also augurs spectacular success and great celebrity. But as a star does not symbolize happiness, it is something of a mixed blessing.

Like the other lines of the palms, the Sun lines may be negatively affected by defects such as bars, islands and breaks. Depending on their size and number, their presence robs the Sun lines of much or all of their promise.

Bar lines symbolize obstacles which temporarily prevent the attainment of fame or which, if the Sun line does not proceed beyond them, blight the career.

An island appearing on the Sun line represents a period of financial difficulty and the notoriety that this attracts. It can sometimes also indicate a scandal and the loss of reputation that this brings. If more than one island or a chain is found on the right-hand Sun line they signify a succession of disasters and much unhappiness.

A break in the Sun line represents a sudden fall from grace, whereby the career is severely damaged and public good will lost. If the break is associated with a bar line then outside factors cause the upset, but if not and if the hand reveals character weaknesses, the person concerned is responsible for his or her misfortunes.

On some hands the Apollo mount bears a line that runs down from the base of the third finger. In India this line is known as the *Vidya rekha* or line of learning. It represents academic success and hence is most commonly found on the hands of distinguished scholars. In its best form it should extend to below the Heart line and be straight and unbroken.

The Lines of Mercury

The Mercury or Health lines, or the *Via Hepaticae*, are vertical lines which run up to the mounts of Mercury from lower down in the palms. Their normal starting point is the mounts of the Moon, although they may rise from the Life lines or the Plains of Mars. They should be straight and clearly marked, free of islands and other defects, and terminate on the mounts of Mercury. However, they are absent on about fifty per cent of hands.

It is a good sign from a health point of view when the Mercury lines are not present, as this indicates that the constitution is strong and the health excellent. It is also favourable for them to be long, straight and well formed because this likewise signifies constitutional strength. Health problems are represented by Mercury lines that are deficient in some way.

As their Latin name—the *Via Hepaticae* or Liver lines—suggests, the Mercury lines symbolize the condition and vitality of your body's most important organ, the liver. And because the liver, in addition to breaking down waste substances and redundant red blood cells, produces bile, which plays an important role in digestion, the Mercury lines also reflect your digestive efficiency. In this respect they should be interpreted in conjunction with the mounts of Venus, which also symbolize the digestion of food and its metabolism.

But while the absence of Mercury lines is a good sign where the health is concerned, it is better if they are present in a well-developed form as this not only signifies good health, but success in business or science, or in some other area of activity ruled by Mercury.

Ideally, the Mercury lines, when present, should start low down on the mounts of the Moon, where their beginning corresponds to your health at birth. They should then proceed to and terminate high up on the mounts of Mercury, their ending corresponding to your demise. Your left-hand Mercury line symbolizes your health and business potential, while that of your right hand represents what you make of these. If you have already determined from your right-hand Life line (and perhaps from its Heart line) the age to which you will live, then those periods of illness that are indicated by any breaks, islands and other defects in the right-hand Mercury line can easily be dated from their position in the line. In this respect they should match similar defects in the Life line, which also refer to health setbacks.

It is not favourable for the Mercury lines to start from the Life lines, a commencement suggesting defective health, or if they rise from the Plains of Mars, which indicates that the health in childhood and youth was poor. But if the lines that rise from these starting points are themselves clearly marked, straight and free from defects, especially that of the right hand, then the inherited health weakness or the early health difficulties will not have a long-term negative effect on the health. However, should the Mercury lines follow a wavy or meandering course from whatever starting point in the palms, this indicates liver and digestive problems and a rheumatic tendency. Wavy Mercury lines also portend a troubled business life.

As with the other vertically rising palm lines, the Mercury lines are more fortunate in meaning if they are branched, the branches symbolizing first-class health and exceptional business, scientific or academic success. It is most propitious if a branch travels to each of the other finger mounts, but because such good fortune in health and business is rarely encountered, so also are three long and clearly marked branch lines. When a single branch line rises to the mount of Jupiter in the right hand it indicates the acquisition of power or authority, successful leadership and the achievement of one's business ambitions. If a branch line from the right-hand Mercury line travels to the Saturn mount, it reveals that business success is gained through hard work, honesty and sensible application. And when a line branches from the right-hand Mercury line to the mount of Apollo, it signifies shrewdness, intellectual brilliance, fame and success.

The age at which success is achieved or at least begun is represented by the point at which the branch or branches leave the right-hand Mercury line. A branch starting low down on the Mercury line symbolizes the early attainment of success, whereas one rising higher on the line refers to success that is gained later in life. It must, however, be remembered that the fortune suggested by such branch lines will only be fully enjoyed if the right-hand Mercury line is long, straight, clearly marked and free from defects.

Those defects that are present in the lines should be carefully examined and evaluated. A break in the right-hand Mercury line represents a sudden and serious health setback, which will relate either to liver or digestive disorders or to other physical problems if there are accompanying negative signs elsewhere in the hands. Such a setback lasts for as long as the break does. Overlapping breaks are symbolic of less serious health upsets, suggesting as they do that the difficulty is naturally overcome, as are any breaks that are surrounded by a square formation. Squares are protective signs and lessen the significance of any defect they surround in the hands. Islands likewise represent periods of ill-

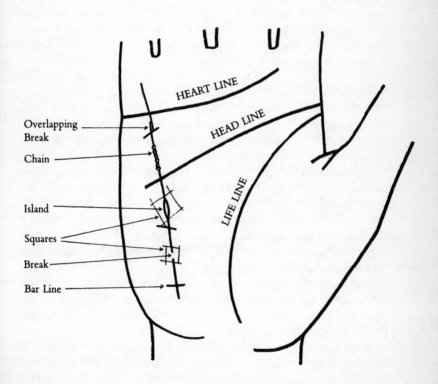

Figure 33

health, although ones that happen more gradually than those symbolized by a break. The island's size and length respectively indicate the magnitude of the health problem and its duration. Bar lines signify outside negative factors which either threaten the health or impede one's business progress. When a bar line coincides with a break it represents an accident, and when a bar line cuts through an island it signifies the strain that causes the health breakdown. These Mercury line defects and the protective squares that may surround them are shown in Figure 33.

When the right-hand Mercury line thins at any point this represents a weakening of the vitality and, as a consequence, a more delicate period of health. Sometimes the Mercury line is clearly marked at the start but later thins out or fades away completely, which naturally indicates that the good health enjoyed in childhood will not be maintained. Or, conversely, a Mercury line which is thin at its origin may become more clearly marked higher up the palm. This suggests that the health improves as the years go by.

The Marriage Lines
The Marriage lines, when they are present, are small transverse lines which lie on the side of the hands between the base of the fourth fingers and the start of the Heart lines, and which run onto the Mercury mounts. There may be one, two, three or more on each hand, which is not surprising because they traditionally presage the number of marriages that we have. Their placement and general form are shown in Figure 34.

But although they are short in length, the Marriage lines, like the other palm lines that signify our interaction with others, should be straight, well-marked, pink in colour and free from breaks and other defects. Any deviance from this ideal form represents some deficiency in the love relationship that each line symbolizes.

Indeed, 'Love Relationship line' would be a better name than 'Marriage line', especially today when so many couples are living together, because although each line signifies a serious emotional involvement, such relationships do not always end in marriage. In fact a marriage should only be predicted if the Marriage line under consideration is both strongly marked and accompanied by other indicators of a union, like a line rising from the right-hand Moon mount to the Fate line. The hand shape is also important in this respect. Those with Earth or Water hands, who tend to be conservative and emotionally dependent, are more likely to solemnize their relationships than people with Fire or Air hands, who are rather unconventional in their attitudes and behaviour. The presence of a ring of Solomon on the right-hand mount of Jupiter is

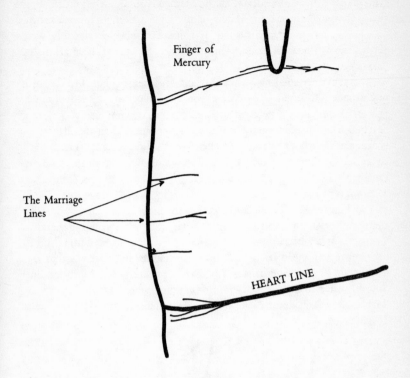

Finger of
Mercury

The Marriage
Lines

HEART LINE

Figure 34

similarly significant. Known as the line of renunciation in India, it
represents a turning away from the world and a rejection of material
values, and as such often suggests a disinclination to marry. This is why it
is often found in the hands of those who have taken religious vows.

Because the distance between the start of the Heart line and the base
of the fourth finger represents a time-span of seventy-five years, it is
very easy to date when the involvement signified by a Marriage line will
take place. A line placed half-way between the Heart line and the base of
the fourth finger symbolizes an affair that happens at about age thirty-
seven and a half, while lines lying below this mid-point refer to earlier
love relationships and those above it to later involvements.

The length of the Marriage line symbolizes the length of time that
love is felt for the person concerned. A short line naturally signifies a
short-lived affair, while a long one, particularly if it is clearly marked,
shows that the affections are centred on the relationship for an extended
period of time. This explains why, if you had a youthful love affair that

still gives you an emotional twinge when you think about it, it is probably represented by a 'Marriage line' of some length in your hands.

The Marriage lines of your left hand symbolize possible love relationships; those of your right hand represent actual love affairs or marriages.

When a Marriage line is thin at its commencement but then deepens and broadens, it symbolizes a corresponding deepening of the feelings as the affair develops (line A in Figure 35). But if, conversely, a clearly marked Marriage line gradually becomes thinner, then the affections weaken as time goes by (line B). The strongest love union is represented by a Marriage line that starts as two lines which merge to form a straight, uniformly marked line that runs onto the Mercury mount (line C).

Sometimes small branches rise upwards from a Marriage line (line D in the Figure 36). These are positive in meaning as they symbolize the emotional and spiritual uplift that the relationship generates. Contrariwise, when branch lines descend from a Marriage line (line E) they represent the difficulties, disappointments and sorrows that the love affair or marriage causes. An island appearing in a Marriage line (line F) refers to a period of emotional unhappiness, which lasts for as long as the island does. A break in a Marriage line (line G) signifies a

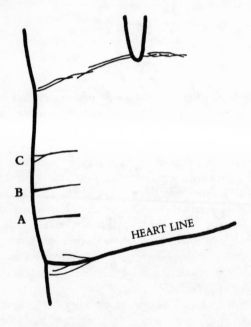

Figure 35

separation that happens suddenly and traumatically. A Marriage line that ends in a fork symbolizes a relationship that drifts apart (line H).

It is never a good sign if a Marriage line bends downwards, particularly if it droops to touch the Heart line, as this symbolizes the loss of the partner through death. Nor is it favourable if a Marriage line is cut by a bar line or terminates in a star or a cross. These signs signify problems which adversely affect the relationship and which may bring about its dissolution, the bar line symbolizing an obstacle that threatens the stability of the union, the star a sudden and dramatic upset, and the cross infidelity.

Short vertical lines rising from one or more of the Marriage lines symbolize children, the longer and thicker ones representing boys, the shorter and thinner ones girls.

Where children are concerned, the appearance of the start of the Heart lines is important. If they begin as a series of short lines, as shown in Figures 35 and 36, this betokens fertility, while if they commence as a single line this signifies low fertility or infertility. You are of course more likely to have children if you possess Heart lines of the first type, although if your hands show other markings indicative of children, such as the islands in the lowermost line circling the thumbs, then it is highly likely that you will have one or more.

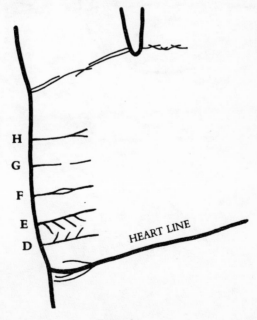

Figure 36

The Girdles of Venus

The Girdles of Venus are semicircular lines that begin between the index and second fingers, curve across the mounts of Saturn and Apollo, and terminate between the third and fourth fingers. They are by no means found on every pair of hands, which is just as well because they symbolize certain emotional and psychological difficulties. Their position and characteristic form is shown in Figure 37.

But the Girdles of Venus are not always marked as clearly as this. Sometimes each consists of a number of shorter lines, which gives them a broken appearance, or they may be formed by two or three lines running together side by side. But whatever their type they can be regarded as sister lines to the Heart lines, which naturally links them with our emotional and sexual nature. Hence their name.

The Girdles of Venus symbolize a higher than normal level of sexual energy and, in turn, a preoccupation with sex. For some people who possess them, particularly if they have Fire hands, this may result in wanton or lascivious behaviour, and, as a consequence, a rather low lifestyle. Indeed, the Girdles of Venus always indicate a fascination with

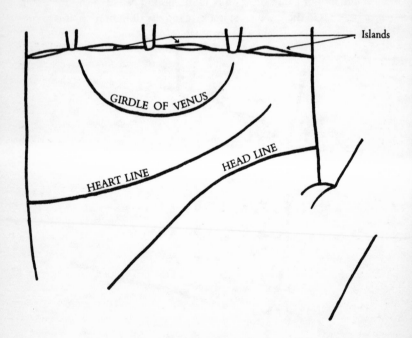

Figure 37

the seedy side of life, and this is why they are commonly found in the hands of drug addicts, pimps and prostitutes. When present in hands that have overdeveloped mounts of Venus and Mars, thick thumbs, and which have islands lying in the basal joint lines of the fingers, as shown in Figure 37, these symbolizing a highly sexed nature, these features represent a person who has great difficulty in controlling his desires. Such a man will be a seducer or, at worst, a rake or rapist.

10

FORTUNATE SIGNS AND MARKINGS

Throughout this book frequent mention has been made of those signs in the hands, such as the island, break and bar line, which affect the palm and finger lines, and the transverse line and grid, which lie on the mounts or on the phalanges of the fingers, that are generally negative in meaning. Indeed, they are called defects. We must now consider in

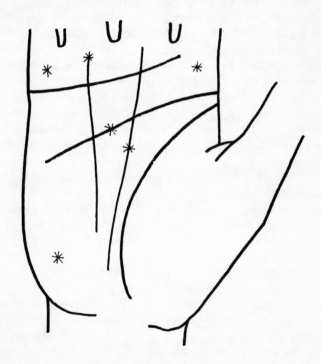

Figure 38

some detail those signs that are generally positive and which, when they are present, presage better luck and fortune.

Three of these more fortunate signs, the star, the trident and the square, we have already encountered, albeit briefly, but there are also the triangle, the fish, the tree, the flag and the temple.

A **STAR** is formed by a series of short lines radiating from a common centre and may either appear as an independent formation or be located in or at the end of one or more of the palm lines (see Figure 38).

The life events that the star refers to are always of a spectacular nature, although they are not by any means always fortunate, and even when the star's placement in the hand is generally positive in meaning there are sometimes drawbacks attached to it. Hence the presence of a star is often a mixed blessing.

When a star lies on a palm mount and is not associated with any of the lines running to the mount, it indicates that special success will be gained in those areas of life linked with the mount. The mounts of Jupiter, for example, are symbolic of our ambitions and our ego needs, and when they are well formed reveal that we have both a desire to further ourselves and better than average luck in fulfilling our ambitions. But when the mounts of Jupiter bear a star this shows that our success will be exceptional and that, along with a high position, some honour or distinction will be gained. A star appearing on the left-hand Jupiter mount reveals the potential for gaining extraordinary success, while a star on the right-hand Jupiter mount shows that such success will be attained. However, a star on the left-hand Jupiter mount does represent inherited good luck, which is a most fortunate quality to have.

A star situated on the mounts of Saturn signifies the development of wisdom or exceptional sagacity and hence, through the proper use of such good sense, the honour and regard of one's fellows. But again, a star must be located on the right-hand Saturn mount for the honour to be earned. When present on the mounts of Apollo, a star promises the achievement of wealth and fame through the exploitation of one's artistic or creative talents. A star on the left-hand Apollo mount symbolizes inborn brilliance, and a star situated on the right-hand Apollo mount shows that such brilliance is successfully utilized. And when a star lies on the mounts of Mercury it presages outstanding success in either business, science, politics or in any field ruled by Mercury. A star on the left-hand Mercury mount symbolizes the potential for achieving this success and a star lying on the right-hand Mercury mount reveals its actual or incipient attainment.

When a star lies on the right-hand mount of Lower Mars it promises success and distinction as a soldier, sailor or airman, or in some field of activity like sport that requires energetic activity. A star placed on the right-hand mount of Upper Mars, which betokens our degree of determination, shows that success and honour will be gained through the exercise of great courage and steadfastness. A star on the right-hand Moon mount indicates that unusual success will be gained through the use of the imagination, as by writing, for example, a work of literary excellence. And when a star is found on the right-hand mount of Venus it reveals great charm and sex appeal and hence much success with the opposite sex and in affairs of the heart.

If a star appears in or at the end of any of the four main vertical lines of the hands, namely, the lines of Jupiter, Saturn, Apollo and Mercury, it is, as we have already seen, a generally fortunate marking. But when a star appears in or terminates any of the three main lines that cross or descend the palms, that is, the Head, Heart and Life lines, it is not a fortunate indication because it symbolizes a sudden and usually detrimental upset in the function of the body part or parts represented by the lines.

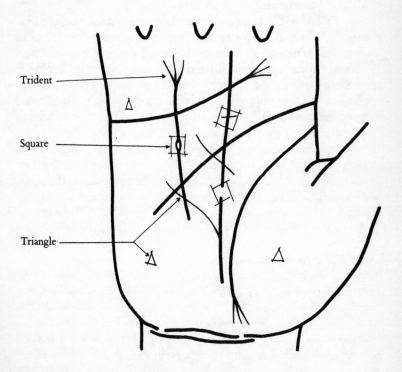

Figure 39

The **TRIDENT** is usually formed by the end of a palm line splitting into three branches (see Figure 39). It is always an excellent marking to have because it adds greatly to the overall meaning of the line it graces. It is in fact a better marking than the star for while it does not symbolize such sudden and unusual success, it does signify greater happiness from what is attained. And unlike the star, the trident is a favourable ending to the lines of Head, Heart and Life. Indeed, it is a mark of outstanding good fortune when the Heart lines terminate in a trident on the mounts of Jupiter. Remarkable intellectual powers are revealed by Head lines that end in a trident, and when a trident terminates the Life lines they symbolize success in later life, a dignified and happy old age, and a peaceful death.

The **SQUARE** is a protective marking and is most positive in meaning when it surrounds a defect like a break or island, thereby indicating that one is spared the worst effects of the illness or accident that the defect represents, which may mean that one's life is preserved. A square situated on a mount neutralizes any deficiencies that the mount may show (see Figure 39).

The **TRIANGLE** is sometimes formed in the hands by three lines crossing, yet it is more fortunate in meaning when it appears as an independent marking. A triangle is, however, always a fortunate sign.

When a triangle is situated on the left-hand mount of Jupiter it symbolizes a stable and mature mind, the power of command, and honest and upright ambitions. If a triangle lies on the right-hand Jupiter mount it indicates that those qualities are applied to the affairs of life and that, as a result, respect and honour are gained through them.

A triangle located on the left-hand Saturn mount signifies an inborn interest in metaphysical and mystical matters, an even and gentle temperament, and a love of the outdoors. When present on the right-hand Saturn mount, a triangle betokens the development of a caring, concerned personality and the achievement of spiritual success.

A triangle located on either the left-hand Apollo mount or Mercury mount symbolizes mental astuteness, which is turned into artistic success when a triangle is found on the right-hand Apollo mount and into business, scientific or political success when a triangle is placed on the right-hand Mercury mount. Such success will be handled well and happiness gained from it.

When a triangle lies on either of the mounts of Lower Mars it indicates a steady application of enthusiasm, great presence of mind and general good fortune. And if a triangle is situated on one or both of the mounts of Upper Mars, it symbolizes correctly channelled persistence and the attainment thereby of success.

A triangle placed on the left-hand mount of the Moon is a sign of an excellent and creative imagination, which will be put to successful practical use if it is accompanied by a triangle on the right-hand Moon mount (see Figure 39).

Lastly, a triangle sited on the mounts of Venus reveals that the sexual or amatory urges are kept under control and are directed towards the establishment of successful, loving relationships. Such triangles are therefore the mark of a mature and responsible individual.

The rather strangely-named signs of the tree, the fish, the flag and the temple are derived from Hindu palmistry and are not widely known in the West.

However, we have already considered, but not yet identified, the sign of the **TREE**, which is formed when two or more branch lines rise from one or other of the vertical palm lines (see Figure 40).

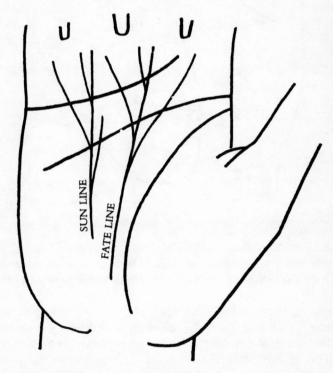

Figure 40

Just as a real tree produces fruit, so the sign of the tree represents success in that area of life symbolized by the vertical line from which it is formed. For example, a tree derived from the right-hand Fate line presages career success. Generally speaking, a tree is a mark of fame, high position, wealth and good fortune.

The sign of the **FISH** is created when a palm line divides into two branches which then travel on for some distance (see Figure 41).

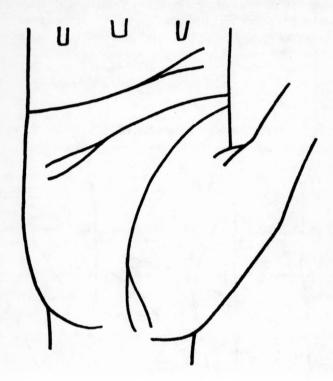

Figure 41

The fish typically appears at the end of the Life lines but it is often also found at the ends of the Head and Heart lines. Indian palmists regard the fish very highly and read much into it, believing it to be a mark of wealth and scholastic success. When a fish is placed on the mounts of Jupiter, where it is usually formed by the Heart lines dividing, it symbolizes power, eminence, honour, religious principles and respect. The fish promises good fortune throughout life when it is found at the end of the right-hand Life line.

The sign of the **FLAG** is attached to the side of one or more of the main palm lines and usually has the appearance shown in Figure 42.

While the flag can represent wealth and success, it more frequently signifies faith, resoluteness, purity of heart and mind and a desire for

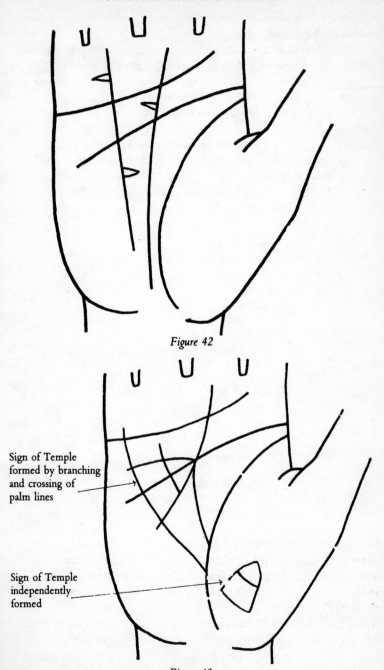

Figure 42

Sign of Temple
formed by branching
and crossing of
palm lines

Sign of Temple
independently
formed

Figure 43

spiritual knowledge. It is often seen in the hands of those who are spiritually advanced.

The **TEMPLE** is a rare and complex mark which betokens the attainment of eminence through wealth, holiness or by virtue of good works. It is an excellent sign wherever it appears on the hands (see Figure 43).

However, these signs and markings should not be interpreted so promisingly if they are found on hands that are otherwise deficient. For while they may represent a neutralization of the deficiencies, they will not augur outstanding success. This can only be predicted if they are found on hands that are also blessed with well-proportioned mounts, straight fingers, good nails and clearly marked, defect-free palm lines.

11

THE CHANGING HANDS

We have now identified the most important hand features and seen how they can be interpreted from a psychological, health and fortune point of view. If you have read this book through from the beginning and have at the same time examined your own hands, you will now have a good idea of what they say about your character, talents, health and longevity, and your marriage and success prospects.

The most fortunate hands, whatever their basic shape, have vigour, strength and a good colour; they have straight fingers, strong and flexible thumbs, and well shaped nails; their mounts are firm and of moderate dimension; the principal lines are clearly marked, long and free from defects; and one or more signs like the triangle, trident or tree are in evidence.

You may have hands like this or you may, at worst, have found little in them to encourage you. If the latter is the case, there is no reason to despair because your hands only reveal your nature and where you are headed at the present moment in time. For the lines and marks of your hands are not carved in stone, they can and do change. Palm lines often fade or strengthen and new ones can appear, just as the mounts can alter their shape and bent or twisted fingers can straighten. You may already have noticed such changes in your hands. If not, you will now probably be aware of them when they do occur.

These changes take place because our future is not immutably fixed. We may not be the masters of our fate, but neither are we puppets dancing to some celestial puppeteer. We exist, in fact, in a state of dynamic interaction with our environment, it influencing us and we influencing it. Limits are imposed upon us by our genetic inheritance – we cannot, for example, become musical geniuses if nature has not given us the necessary mental equipment—but we do have the power to direct our lives to quite a considerable extent. This is why history provides us with so many instances of men and women who, though born into poor and humble circumstances, rose to greatness through their own efforts.

You may perhaps wish to become wealthy, successful and famous or your hopes for yourself may be much more modest. If you have fortunate hands many of your hopes will be realized. But if not, you need to take stock, redefine your goals and set off on a new path. For fortune favours the brave and will reward those who struggle to better themselves. And such a change in attitude will be reflected in quite marked changes occurring in your hands.

But if you envy those who seem to have more talents and better luck than you do, remember that what one gains on Fortune's swings one may lose on her roundabouts. Alexander the Great, ancient Greece's most brilliant military commander, died a drunk at age thirty-two; Wolfgang Mozart, composer of some of the world's most sublime music, was buried in a pauper's grave at age thirty-six; and Elvis Presley, the golden boy of rock 'n' roll, became a hopeless drug addict and dropped dead in his bathroom at age forty-two. Their lives, though spectacular in many respects, were short and unhappy.

The imprisoned Boethius imagined Fortune saying to him:

Inconstancy is my very essence, it is the game I never cease to play as I turn my wheel in its ever changing circle, filled with joy as I bring the top to the bottom and the bottom to the top. Yes, rise up on my wheel if you like, but don't count it an injury when by the same token you begin to fall, as the rules of the game will require. You must surely have been aware of my ways . . . Indeed, my very mutability gives you just cause to hope for better things.

Index